THE THREE C'S

A Career Enrichment Primer on Characterizing,
Connecting, and Communicating

MARK A. STONE

WestBow
PRESS
A DIVISION OF THOMAS NELSON

WestBow Press books may be ordered through booksellers or by contacting:

WestBow Press
A Division of Thomas Nelson
1663 Liberty Drive
Bloomington, IN 47403
www.westbowpress.com
1 (866) 928-1240

Because of the dynamic nature of the Internet, any web addresses or links contained in this book may have changed since publication and may no longer be valid. The views expressed in this work are solely those of the author and do not necessarily reflect the views of the publisher, and the publisher hereby disclaims any responsibility for them.

Material cited from
LOVE IS THE KILLER APP by Tim Sanders, copyright © 2002 by Tim Sanders
New afterword copyright (c) 2003 by Tim Sanders is used by permission
of Crown Business, a division of Random House, Inc. Any third party use
of this material, outside of this publication, is prohibited. Interested
parties must apply directly to Random House, Inc. for permission.

Material cited from NEVER EAT ALONE: AND OTHER SECRETS TO SUCCESS, ONE RELATIONSHIP AT A TIME by Keith Ferrazzi and Tahl Raz, copyright © 2005 by Keith Ferrazzi is used by permission of Doubleday, a division of Random House, Inc. Any third party use of this material, outside of this publication, is prohibited. Interested parties must apply directly to Random House, Inc. for permission.

Any people depicted in stock imagery provided by Thinkstock are models, and such images are being used for illustrative purposes only. Certain stock imagery © Thinkstock.

ISBN: 978-1-4908-1882-5 (sc)
ISBN: 978-1-4908-1881-8 (hc)
ISBN: 978-1-4908-1883-2 (e)

Library of Congress Control Number: 2013922394

Printed in the United States of America.

WestBow Press rev. date: 02/07/2014

To those in transition

CONTENTS

LIST OF ILLUSTRATIONS

Main Text

- o Claims Diagram
- o Oklahoma Land Openings

Appendices

- o Résumé Example A
- o Résumé Example B
- o Résumé Example C
- o Bio Example

LIST OF TABLES

INTRODUCTION

The request was deflating. My boss asked me to develop a plan to reduce IT headcount and IT operating expenses by 20 percent. I knew this was only a contingency plan if company sales dropped 20 percent in the upcoming holiday season. But given it was October, 2008 and I had just executed a 20 percent reduction in force and a 20 percent elimination of IT operating expenses eight months earlier, the request was simply deflating.

Over the next couple of weeks, I worked diligently in solitude. There was no way that I was going to share this with my direct reports and allow the rumor mill to crank back up. I considered multiple scenarios and struggled with the guilt of having to play God again. It is one thing to cut headcount 20 percent--you eliminate PMO, you dismiss many of your project managers (no need for all of them if you don't get capital for projects), you decrease the number of mid-level management positions (Managers and Directors) by combining teams, etc.--but it is something completely different to eliminate a second wave of employees for an on-going concern (even though it was heading toward the verge of bankruptcy). Now you are eliminating capacity, experience, institutional knowledge, and timely production support--and we all know what that means. When and if the business recovers, the company will not be in a position to exploit the recovery. They will find themselves behind their stronger competitors who did not cut too deep. They will find themselves chasing the talent they need (and had) to catch up.

The proposal submitted in November surprised my boss. The proposal included the elimination of my job--the CIO of the company! There was no need for a strategic IT role if the company was going to focus on survival, not innovation. There was no need for a CIO if capital was not going to be made available in the coming year. There was no need for a CIO if IT was going into maintenance mode. IT resources that focused on production support, break-fix, POS, regulatory enhancements, privacy, security, and PCI requirements were much more critical.

Before you come to the conclusion that I was a martyr (that urban legend had to be snuffed out in the months after I departed), I recognized I stood a better chance to control my destiny if I left on my terms. My employment agreement stated that severance would be paid out on a monthly basis, not in a lump sum. Given that a 20 percent decrease in sales during the 2008 holiday season combined with any double-digit decrease in the next holiday season would push the company to the edge of bankruptcy, I chose to leave early (rather than later) enough to get most of my severance. Secondly, there was no advantage in staying another year since nothing of any value would be added to my résumé.

Sure enough, year over year sales dropped 19.6 percent during the critical 2008 holiday season. Much of January was spent finalizing the "plan." And during the last week of January, 2009, I personally told twenty IT employees their services were no longer required. One week later, it was announced to the company, I would also be leaving. And so began my journey through that dreaded phase called--in transition. You know, that time in your life when you:

- o   No longer can call oneself the CFO of ABC, Inc.
- o   Wake up and wonder what you are going to do with your day.
- o   Have to explain why you are unemployed.
- o   Realize for the first time that the job market (and the new skills required) has left you behind.
- o   Fear being offered a good job--in California (only non-Californians understand this fear).
- o   Realize that you are no longer in control (or in charge).
- o   Wonder if you will ever find a new job.

That was the Situation!

You would think since I had known for three months that my job might be going away, I would have been better prepared. You might even think given my lengthy service (fourteen years) in the retail industry, I would have been in demand. You are wrong! I naively began the in transition phase of my life totally unprepared!

- o   I could not articulate my value proposition.
- o   I had a ridiculously small and weak network.
- o   I did not know how to interview.
- o   I had even underestimated the difficulty the recession of 2009 would pose for any and all IT executives in transition.
- o   Simply put--I was in over my head!

Not wanting to throw in the towel, I chose to knuckle down. I:

- o   Met with my personal outplacement coach. Forty-five seconds into my first practice interview, I held up my hands to signal "time out." I told him: "That is one of the worst answers that I have ever heard to a ridiculously easy question. I obviously need help in learning how to interview."
- o   Joined several support groups. By the time I had met with each of the three groups, three times, I found myself hearing the same advice and same counsel.
- o   Re-wrote my résumé multiple times only to have another "expert" re-write the resume again.
- o   Made a list of every person in my network. It took me about two weeks to burn through that list.
- o   Posted for over a hundred jobs only to hear back in writing from three.
- o   Read everything that had been written on being in transition. The information proved to be confusing and contradictory.

It was then, that I threw up my hands. Nothing was working! Worse, I was scared.

You may challenge that conclusion given I was only sixty days removed from my job of the previous fourteen years. You may chastise me for being impatient. But what you don't know is that sixty days into this new phase of my life, I was directionless and clueless. I was merely running around with my head cut off--applying for every job that even remotely looked like me, uncertain of which version of my résumé I had submitted, and meeting with people who had great intentions but no idea how to help me. I desperately needed to recalibrate!

That was the Complication!

In his book, *The Circle of Innovation*, Tom Peters wrote about the white-collar revolution. He believed that a confluence of factors-- including a streamlining of business processes, technology that replaces jobs, an increase in outsourcing to foreign countries, and an age of entrepreneurialism where more and more people see themselves as free agents--were combining in such a way that over 90 percent of all white-collar jobs would be radically different or would not exist at all in ten to fifteen years. [Tom Peters, *Circle of Innovation: You Can't Shrink Your Way to* Greatness, p. 158] Whether it is outsourcing to foreign countries, increased productivity from new mobility devices, or the inexorable movement to cloud computing--the nature and number of white-collar jobs are changing.

While the timing of his prediction may have been premature, it is apparent that many of these factors were beginning to impact the world that I was now entering as I searched for my next job. How was I going to find a job in this new marketplace? What was I going to do to survive in this new economic order? As Keith Ferrazzi writes: "Our careers aren't paths so much as landscapes that need to be navigated." [Keith Ferrazzi, *Never Eat Alone: And Other Secrets to Success, One Relationship At a* Time, p. 17]

While I do not have the complete answers to these questions, I would like to provide you with a primer on how to build, enhance, and protect your career. This primer is the product of what I learned in 2009 and what has been shared with hundreds of individuals on a one-on-one basis since then. This plan of action--<u>characterizing, connecting, and communicating</u>--is not the best plan. It is not the only plan. It is just a proven plan.

That was the Answer!

SECTION

1 Characterizing (Creating Your Brand)

The first lesson I learned in transition was the importance of branding one self. If I were to place a swoosh in front of you, how many of you would struggle to identify it as belonging to Nike? If you saw a billboard with black and white-spotted cows (whether or not there was any writing), how many of you would immediately know that the billboard belongs to Chick-fil-A? If you were parachuted into a pro football stadium and one team had blue stars on a silver helmet, how many of you would not think that you were watching the Dallas Cowboys?

As a technology professional, I'm keenly aware that image and identity have become increasingly important in our new economic order. With the information marketplace drowning in sameness, a powerful brand-- built not on a degree or product but on a personal message--has become a competitive necessity. [Ferrazzi, p. 224] Stated differently, the bottom line for everyone comes down to a choice: "to be distinct or extinct." [Ferrazzi, p. 226]

Practically speaking--how does one brand oneself? What does a personal branding statement look like? How is a brand statement used? To answer these and other questions, it will be helpful to provide you with an overview of where we are going. Then we will de-construct a sample brand statement and show how one creates a unique brand statement.

OVERVIEW

Your brand statement should be a simple, concise statement of who you are and what you do best. For example: "I am a financially-savvy marketer who uses social media to drive customer advocacy." This brand statement is less than fifteen words and it rolls off the tongue very easily.

Your brand statement should also make at least three pregnant claims. Notice that the sample brand statement uses three very powerful terms (or phrases)--financially-savvy, social media, and customer advocacy. Each of these phrases creates an image, makes a statement, and says a lot with little definition needed.

The claims you make in your brand statement should answer these questions--Who are you? What do you do best? The claims should be real, relevant, and should resonate with those you speak with. They should also capture in a few words/phrases your very essence--your DNA.

How and why you chose to make those claims, will be seen by looking at those things that make you up--your experiences, skills, jobs, degrees, talents, certificates, passions, interests, and hobbies. Each of us possesses a unique set of experiences, skills, etc. that define who we are and what we do best.

WHO IS THE OWNER OF YOUR BRAND?

Before we begin the process of building your brand statement, it is important to answer the question: "Who is the owner of your brand?" The answer is "*you*"! You cannot expect someone else to define who you are. You cannot depend upon someone else to influence other people's personal and professional expectations of who you are. Your career is yours and yours alone to manage. Your career requires work. It requires that you put a lot of sweat equity into building and managing it.

WHO ARE YOU?

So how do you create an identity for a successful career? How do you become the swoosh of your company? Of your network? The first step in building a brand is to define who you are. That is because a brand is nothing less than everything everyone thinks of when they see or hear your name. [Ferrazzi, p. 228] This step requires that you make a self-assessment of yourself. To assist you in understanding how this works, let's go back to the example used earlier in this chapter and see how our marketing veteran built her brand statement. The first thing she did was to conduct a self-assessment.

Self-Assessment Worksheet

1. What degrees do you have?
   I graduated with a bachelor's degree in marketing. While I was working at my first job, I completed an MBA at night (and on the weekends) with an emphasis in finance.

2. What jobs have you held?
   I worked for four different companies. After completing college, I went to work for an ad agency. Three years later, I got a great opportunity to work in the marketing department of a large, global consumer package goods ("CPG") company. A CPG competitor hired me away five years later only to see me jump to one of the large social media web site companies.

3. What types of experience do you have?
   I learned the nuts and bolts of advertising at the ad agency. I held two different roles at the global CPG firm. One required me to build a brand image for one of their products and work to retain customer loyalty in that product. The other required me to review proposals by external companies who were pitching their services to assist the CPG in firm managing brand marketing in Latin America. At the rival CPG firm, I did much of the same work but moved from personal care items to snacks and soft drinks. My final role at the large social media firm enabled me to work with potential advertisers who wanted to use social media to influence product and service selection.

4. What skills have you acquired?
   In addition to understanding advertising, I have held roles that required me to use marketing, finance, and contracting skills. I was known as one who could wear many hats and was well suited to serve as a product owner. Finally, I learned the intricacies and nuances of the latest wave in marketing – social media marketing.

5. What are you passionate about?
   Having placed ads for clients with TV stations, radio stations, and newspapers and having seen search marketing come and go--I am passionate about advertising via social media. I believe that I understand how one can unlock that medium to turn customers into followers, followers into fans, and fans into marketers.

6. What hobbies do you have?
   I am proud to tell you that I have had a MySpace account before most knew what it was. I was one of Facebook's first 100,000 accounts and have since experimented with every new, major social networking site. I am fascinated with this medium and am an expert in telling you each site's strengths and weaknesses.

Like this marketer, you need to make a self-assessment. You need to write down everything you have done, everything you have accomplished, and everything you are interested in. You need to organize them into the categories shown in the diagram doing your best to be specific and realistic.

WHAT DO YOU DO BEST?

Having completed a self-assessment, it is time to evaluate what you do best. This is a really important question to answer, because this is often the first question (or a variation of it) that interviewers ask.

I have asked this question of every single person I have met with whether they were in transition or seeking career advice. Many just look at me with that deer-in-the-headlights look (I am from Texas and I have seen that look in the middle of the night, in the Hill Country, way too many times). They freeze and usually mumble, "That is a really good question." Others (like the time I answered my outplacement coach) begin listing off three-to-five qualities over the next three-to-five minutes. "I am good at aligning business and technology needs..... I am good at taking tough technical problems and explaining them in easy-to-understand non-technical...... Oh, and I am good at...." You get the idea. Rather than making a clear, concise statement of what they do best, they drone on and on expecting the interviewer to navigate through the tidal wave of information to figure out what they do best. Stop!

All of us are good at something. All of us have some combination of experiences, jobs, and degrees that make us better in some roles than in others. It is your job, not the interviewer's, to sift through your experiences, jobs, degrees, skills, passions, interests, hobbies, etc. and boil it down to a clear, concise statement of what you do best.

What does our hypothetical marketer do best? The answer is not that simple. Her problem is not that she possesses few skills or strengths. Her problem is that she has a deep résumé and struggles with telling others what she does best in a clear, concise manner. Her brand statement must possess multiple claims. It should have at least three claims but probably no more than five. (Can anyone really claim there are six or more things they do best?). Which leads us to this question: "What claims do I make?"

WHAT ARE THE QUALITIES OF YOUR CLAIMS?

"April 22, 1889, dawned bright and clear. Surrounding the Unassigned Lands, an estimated fifty thousand people--impoverished farmers, tradesmen, professionals, common laborers, capitalists, and politicians--eagerly looked to the cornucopia of opportunity offered by settlement of the long-withheld lands of the Indian Territory. The 2 million-acre Unassigned Lands, left vacant in the post-Civil War effort to create reservations for Plains Indians and other tribes, were considered some of the best unoccupied public land in the nation. The ink was hardly dry on President Benjamin Harrison's March 23, 1889, proclamation before prospective settlers began hitching their teams to wagons and loading their families and scant worldly goods. Others saddled their fastest horses or caught trains to the place on the border they considered to be the most advantageous point of entry.

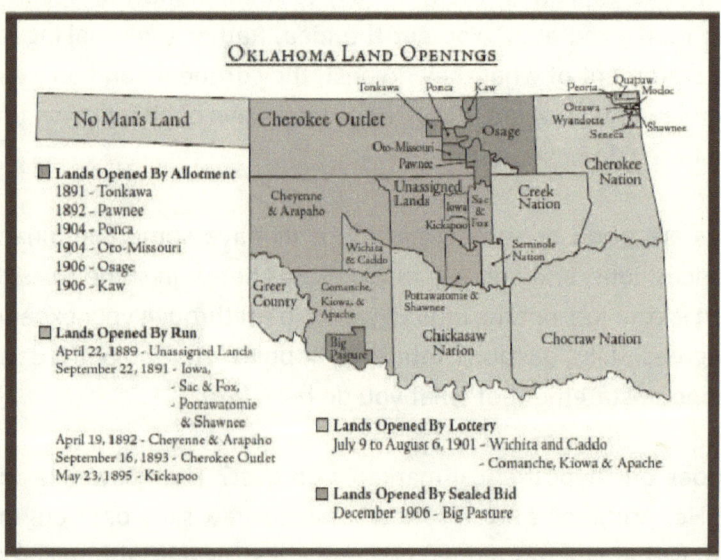

The great dramatic moment came, when at the stroke of noon, starting signals were given at the many points of entry. In some instances it was given by a blue-clad military officer firing his pistol or by his trumpeter, at times by a citizen firing his rifle in the air, or, as at Fort Reno, by the boom of a cannon. All produced the same results--a tumultuous avalanche of wagons and horsemen surging forward all in one breathtaking instant.

Some who made the run sought to beat others to choice homesteads by entering early and hiding out until the legal time of entry. These people came to be known as 'sooners.' The hundreds of legal contests that arose from this practice would be decided first at local land offices, then by the Department of the Interior. Others followed the rules and sprinted to the location of choice.

Families that remained behind at the line cheered as a husband or father made his wild dash to stake his claim. He would then determine its range and township from the surveyors' cornerstone markers and plant a stake bearing notice of his name and location. Some would immediately begin making token improvements such as digging a well or arranging logs for a potential home. Others would hurry to the land office to register their claim. Under the provisions of the Homestead Act of 1862, a legal settler could claim those 160 acres of public land, and those who lived on and improved the claim for five years could receive title to the land--all at no cost!" [Oklahoma Historical Society, *Land Run of 1889*]

Like those who raced into the Unassigned Lands in 1889 to stake a claim for 160 acres of land, you need to determine what claims you can make. These claims should be the result of your self-assessment and state boldly and clearly who you are and what you do best. Or stated differently, you need to build a list of key words/phrases that you want people to think of when referring to you. You want to identify the most important skills and attributes you bring to the table. You want to stake a claim!

When choosing what claims you are going to make, you need to remember three things--your claims need to be relevant, they need to resonate, and they need to be real.

1. Your claims must be relevant.
    First, the claims must be relevant.

    o   An information technology professional -- for example – would
        want to claim <u>database expertise</u> in Microsoft SQL Server or the
        Oracle Developer Suite. He would want to highlight his experience
        in <u>unified communications</u>, messaging systems, VoIP, and/or IP
        telephony, which are among the highest paying IT skills in the
        industry. He would want to highlight his expertise in <u>IT security</u>.
        The value of security skills as evidenced by security certifications-
        -such as the CompTIA Security+, GIAC Security Essentials, Certified
        Ethical Hacker, GIAC Certified Incident Handler and Check Point
        Certified Security Administrator--have increased in value. He
        would want to show his understanding and experience with <u>data</u>
        <u>mining</u> and related fields such as information on demand, content
        management and unstructured information management. He
        would not want to claim Lotus Notes or WordPerfect expertise
        as these are irrelevant. Nor would he want to normally claim
        that he is an expert in Peoplesoft Financials or waterfall project
        management as these are skill sets of another decade.
    o   A marketing professional – for example – would want to claim that
        she has acquired skills in <u>analytical pattern recognition</u>. Marketing
        is at the center of a data maelstrom, flooded by fire hose-velocity
        feeds of information--web analytics, transaction histories,
        behavioral profiles, industry aggregates, social community
        feedback, etc. Wrangling the flow of that data is a good skill, as is
        proficiency with tools such as Excel and Google Analytics. However,
        the real skill to have is the ability to look beyond the numbers to
        see the underlying patterns and trends--to coax out explanations
        and ideas from the endless sea of bits. She would want to claim
        that she has deep experience with <u>agile project management</u>. The
        clock speed of marketing is accelerating, while the granularity of
        its tactics is fragmenting. The luxurious days of planning a few well-
        contained major campaigns for the year are largely gone. Now,
        you've got hundreds--often thousands--of micro-opportunities,
        swirling around the extended enterprise every week, the best

of which must be quickly snatched and efficiently executed. Priorities can change overnight, and near instantaneous social media feedback demands a near instantaneous response. Old school project planning can't keep up in that environment. You need agile marketing. Agile methodologies, originally invented for rapid software development, are now being successfully adapted for use in the marketing department such as a Scrum approach to marketing. She would want to claim expertise in mashable software fluency. Not all marketers have to become programmers, but those who understand how software is built and deployed in the new mashable web--a world of mashups, widgets, and API's – will have a competitive advantage. She would not want to claim that she has significant database marketing or mass media experience as these are skill sets of the past. [Scott Brinker, *Five New Skills for the Future of Marketing*]

o   A supply chain leader--for example--would want to claim he understands the complete supply chain. In a consumer food supply chain, this would refer to all activities that take place from "farm gate" to "consumer plate." In a manufacturing supply chain, it would refer to all processes from initial sourcing of raw materials through to product manufacture and value-adding activities that take place up to the point where the product reaches its final destination. A supply chain professional would want to claim that he is experienced across all major aspects of the end-to-end supply chain. Traditionally in a retail supply chain, for instance, the supply chain leader would likely have spent his full career in the retail section of the chain and have little direct experience in other key areas. Future leaders will have spent periods of their careers in manufacturing, logistics/ distribution and retail. Such a broad level of experience and exposure will make them much better qualified to understand the full chain, identify potential risks and, therefore, address issues effectively as they arise. A supply chain professional would want to claim that he has experience living and working in multiple regions and cultures in both developed and emerging markets. In light of the growing impact of emerging economies on industries and organizations worldwide, it is clear future supply chain leaders need to understand intimately the challenges involved in operating in geographies with different socio-economic backgrounds.

Relevant claims are simply those that are valued in this new economic order. Relevant claims are those employers need. Relevant claims are those that address future job targets. When making claims, choose those that are relevant.

2. Your claims must resonate with others.
    Second, your claims must resonate with others. When others think of this claim, the claim should be so simple, a single word (or a short phrase) is all that is needed to describe this claim. Much like a stone cast into a pond or a tuning fork that is struck but one time, your claim needs to resonate in the minds of others long after it is presented. Read job board postings to learn what is in demand, to learn what are the key words. Words and phrases such as "mobility", "SOX", "social media", "SAP", "unified communications", "data mining", "analytical pattern recognition", "agile methodology", "global supply chain", and "transformational" resonate. Each of them strikes a chord and causes others (potential employers, supervisors, etc.) to immediately grasp how your claim is important and how it impacts them. They are rich with meaning and--while each person's understanding may differ slightly--create an immediate picture of who you are.

    o   An information professional--for example--would want to use the term "mobility" rather than "telephone systems." He would want to use the term "SAP" rather than "ERP system." He would want to use the term "data mining" rather than "database analyst."
    o   A marketing professional--for example--would want to incorporate the term "analytical pattern recognition" into her brand statement rather than "marketing analytics." She would want to use "agile methodology" rather than "project manager." She would want to use the term "social media" rather than "print advertising."
    o   A supply chain leader--for example--would want to use the term "global supply chain" rather than "retail supply chain." He would

want to use the term "end-to-end" rather than "broad skills." He would want to use the term "complete supply chain" rather than "from sourcing to manufacturing."

The claims you make need to resonate.

3. Your claims must be real.
    Third, your claims must be real. It makes no sense to make a claim that is untrue and/or unsupportable. To authenticate your claim, you need to be able to identify three-to-five success stories that support each claim. These success stories must be real examples, drawn from your work experience. They should be crafted in terms of how you increased revenues, decreased expenses, increased efficiencies, and/ or diminished risks. They should be crafted in terms of actual dollars and percentages. They should be concrete, not abstract. It is easy to try and become something you want to be rather than what you are. Don't go down that road. Work diligently to stake claims that are real and supportable.

Let's look back at our hypothetical marketer and see what claims it makes sense for her to make. Claims that are relevant, resonate, and real. In that marketers are largely, by nature, creative and artistic-- one claim she should make is that she is financially-minded. She had spent years reviewing external vendor proposals, determining not only that they made creative sense, but that they delivered a positive return on investment. She also had spent several years showing potential advertisers how social media advertising made financial sense. She had invested her evenings and weekends for almost three years to get an MBA in Finance. It makes sense for her to claim she is "financially-savvy."

A second logical claim was she was knowledgeable about how to use "social media" to influence customer behavior and purchasing patterns. Many in the marketing space like to state they have used social media to influence customer behavior but that experience was usually a small part of their work responsibilities. Most in marketing still have oversight of media buys that include traditional media, search marketing, and to a lesser extent, social media. Our hypothetical marketer had spent years focused on this new marketing phenomenon and could easily claim she is an expert in this nascent field of marketing. It is a real claim that is very relevant. It makes sense for her to weave the term "social media" into her brand statement.

A third claim is arguably the most audacious. The promised land of marketing is not and never has been customer loyalty. The promised land of marketing has always been customer advocacy. Companies want loyal customers but they dream for customers who are advocates for the products and services of the company. Loyal customers continually come back for repetitive sales. Customer advocates create new customers without any effort on your part. How many retailers drool when they go by an Apple store in the mall? How many companies would give their right arm to have the number of customer advocates that Apple has for their iPad's and iPhone's? By making a claim that she is able to drive customer advocacy, she is telling others: 1) she knows the difference between customer loyalty and customer advocacy and 2) she has acquired a skill set that places her in rarified company. That real claim will resonate clearly and loudly with others. It makes sense for her to boldly claim success in creating customer advocates.

WHAT ARE THE SOURCES OF YOUR CLAIMS?

Claims can have their root in a degree, a job, or a series of roles. Let me give you an example. My brand statement is: "I am an innovative, servant-leader that transforms broken and underperforming organizations." Embedded within this brand statement are three claims.

- o   I am innovative.
- o   I am a servant-leader.
- o   I am transformational.

Each of these claims are relevant and resonate with companies in the technology space.

Where did I come up with the claim that I am a servant-leader? There are many servant-leaders who struggle in substantiating such a claim. That is because the concept of servant leadership has both a secular and faith-based definition. While I can recite a handful of success stories that show I am a secular servant-leader, it is much easier for me to point to other aspects of my skill sets and experiences that substantiate a more faith-based definition. Specifically, I can point to my Masters in Divinity, my ordination as a minister, and my years of pastoral ministry that demonstrate servant leadership. Isn't it true that many believe that Jesus Christ was the epitome of a servant leader? And what is better than pointing out your training and ministry in His methods and practical experience in following those methods to substantiate your ability to be a servant leader? Even if it is in the business world!

Where did I come up with the claim I am transformational? This one is much more comical. As I began my in transition state in 2009, I did not think of myself as being transformational. (Note: I had not thought of myself as being anything in particular because that was just not something that needed to be done.) I was instructed by my outplacement coach to craft explanations for my various job and role changes over my career. When one looked at my fourteen years at a specialty goods retailer, a yellow flag went up. I had held six different roles in only fourteen years. Why?

I began to assess why I held so many roles in such a short period of time. I started as the head of the newly created Project Management Office. The IT Department had not had such an Office for years. The processes were broken and the tools non-existent. After less than two years, my team had developed a set of processes and had selected and implemented a set of tools that brought order to chaos. Those tools brought discipline to the disorganized. Those processes brought a repeatable model to a department that succeeded by shear brute force labor rather than by intentional structure. We did not merely improve the magnitude of the processes, we created a fundamentally different kind of process.

The CIO approached me and asked me to assume responsibility over the Stores Team. I was appalled! I had just fixed the PMO and now he was assigning me to a Team that was in disarray! This team had an aged POS system that was held together by bubble gum and shoelaces. The operating system was over twenty years old and had stopped being supported by the manufacturer ten years earlier. To make matters worse, the operating system was so archaic that it would not even run on new equipment. That necessitated us buying computer parts for the hardware from PC junk yards and flea markets in Latin America!

The Stores Team supporting this system had a bunker mentality. Who would blame them? The stores hated the system so much it was painful to hear the frustration, the anger, and the venom from store personnel on calls they made to the Stores Help Desk. The low morale on the Stores Application Team was magnified by the high turnover on the Stores Help Desk--necessitating that the application team had to answer many of the calls themselves.

With the help of a talented team, we migrated the POS system to a new platform. We upgraded the operating system and underlying database to new, supported versions. This new POS platform was rolled out to all 2,000+ stores over an eighteen month period. A new call-tracking system and standardized call answering procedures were implemented. Help desk personnel skills were upgraded to include more technical prowess (to increase the percentage of calls that could be answered by Level 1 team members). We didn't just make the systems and processes--better, cheaper, and faster. We fundamentally created new systems and processes never seen before. The results were stunning! Store down-time decreased by 70 percent. Every help-desk-metric improved by at least 50 percent. Annual turnover went from 27 percent to less than 5 percent.

Sometime in my fifth year, the CIO approached me and told me he was promoting me to head up all applications. I again had to swallow hard because most of the other application teams were not functioning as well as the Stores Team. Retailers are notoriously short on funds for technology and the years of underfunding technology initiatives had resulted in a large number of custom legacy applications that were increasingly difficult and expensive to support. And you can guess what the users felt about these old systems! In that I was getting a promotion in pay and title, this time I was a little more willing to take on the task.

Much like the earlier assignments, I was privileged to have a team that quickly learned how to be successful. In the next three years, the applications teams rolled out new sales audit, distribution, store polling, merchandise planning, and merchandising systems (amongst others). The communication between the business and IT became natural and open. IT was viewed as a collaborative partner who not only understood the needs of the business but quite often possessed more institutional knowledge of business processes than the business itself. This was enhanced by the decision to add ten-year-plus business users into the IT Department to seed the Department with business expertise at the analyst, managerial, and director levels. Most importantly, the IT Department had great credibility with the business community. The improvements were not merely in terms of order of magnitude. Fundamental changes in kind took place.

In my eighth year at the retailer, I was frustrated because there was nothing else to fix. The application teams were running like clockwork (or at least as much as was possible in a specialty-retail IT environment). I was bored. There was work to do but it was not possible to move the company in a major way in a short period of time. The company was somewhat weary of major changes and wanted to slow down the pace of change for a season and direct the capital funds in a different direction.

Fortunately for me, some of those funds were directed to a major acquisition. I saw my chance! I approached the CIO (a different individual from the one who had moved me to the Stores Team and to the head of application development) and asked if I could assume the role over the distribution center of the acquired institution in Pennsylvania.

The distribution center was operating a PC-based system that no one had ever heard of. Freight expenses were spiraling out of control (which is a disaster in a low margin, low turn business). The morale of the staff was at an all-time low due to the acquisition. The staff was convinced we would close the DC and move it to Texas (they were right!). The DC was located in an area hit hard by the closure of Bethlehem Steel years earlier and one that had yet to recover. The inefficient operations made it difficult to distribute goods to the stores on a timely basis. Payroll expenses were increasing just as sales in the brand were declining. I couldn't be more excited to get there!

With the support of the IT Department I had left and the incredibly loyal staff at the DC, we transformed the entire operation. Improved distribution processes were driven by the implementation of the same distribution system used at the mother-ship. Tilt-tray sorter processes were modified to decrease errors, speed up picking, and increase potential picking capacity in an eight-hour day. Receiving and accounting processes related to receipts and transfers were completely re-written and implemented resulting in lower shrinkage, faster DC inventory replenishment, and reduced unnecessary purchases. Morale was rebuilt despite the pending closure of the facility by treating each employee as a valuable resource, instituting monthly meetings, issuing personal notes for birthdays and anniversaries, and involving them in all decision-making matters.

The results were tangible. Annual-freight-charges decreased by 35 percent. Annual payroll expense was reduced by 11 percent. The number of days required to ship goods to all stores was reduced from 3.5 days to 2.5 days. Annual turnover was reduced to approximately 6 percent. Never have I been so sad to say goodbye to a set of employees who gave 100 percent to the very end. And despite our willingness to provide any of them jobs at the new DC in Texas--not a single employee transferred!

Knowing I would be available for a new role after closing down and transferring the DC to Texas, the company had the perfect role for me. A newly centralized, merchandising planning function had just been created. The new seventy-plus team had no standardized processes, systems, or methodologies. The staff was de-moralized due to having been pulled out of their brand (this retailer had seven brands) and many did not like the change in their line of reporting or the change in their role definition.

In-stock and replenishment rates were unacceptable. Each brand had their own way of managing in-stock's and replenishing. Since the company had just made a purchase of a new SKU forecasting and replenishment system, who better to implement it than an IT person with distribution experience?

With the incredible support of the team (a special shout-out to M.G.), we implemented a brand new standard process flow-sheet methodology, a single version of the replenishment system, new in-stock reporting processes, and established brand/SKU forecasting functionality. Within eighteen months, in-stock rates improved to over 90 percent including key items to over 95 percent. The number of hours required to prepare a SKU-level forecast decreased by 50 percent. And annual turnover decreased from a frightening 75 percent to less than 15 percent.

After a tour of duty as the head of Financial Planning & Analysis (which was one of the most valuable roles in my career--thanks M.L.), I returned to the Information Technology Department as the CIO. The situation had deteriorated to such a degree that it was impossible to believe this was the same Department I had left five years earlier. A third CIO had taken the reins of the Department and driven the Department over the cliff. The relationship with the user organizations was completely broken. A major vendor went around the CIO to complain to the CEO. The morale of the staff had deteriorated to the point that turnover was exceeding 25 percent per year. In fact, people took the long way out of the Department to avoid walking by the CIO's office. Worst of all, the IT organization was pushing technological solutions that were not embraced by the business and made no financial sense.

Relying upon many of the staff that had worked with me so faithfully years earlier, IT underwent a radical re-birth. IT was given a seat at the Executive Table. Turnover was reduced to around 4 percent per year. We canceled the major ERP initiative that was technologically and financially the wrong answer. This decision saved the Company from spending at least another $10 million on what would have been a failed system implementation. Instead, the Company was able to implement a demand forecasting and item planning system in less than twelve months. It was also able to redirect the business from a single ERP implementation to more important efforts--remerchandising the stores, reducing inventory, growing the Dot. Com business, etc. In a short period of time, IT overhauled and replaced core merchandising and planning processes.

As I reviewed my career at this retailer, it dawned on me. I was transformational! I loved to fix broken things. And I seemed to be good at it. I also learned I get bored easily. I would rather manage a hell hole than take a well-run organization and turn it into a world-class organization. I simply did not have the patience to make small, incremental changes. I liked to see major changes in a very short period of time. That is how I determined that I was transformational. It was in my DNA.

<u>Where did you come up with your claims? How do you complete a self-assessment?</u> While there are many ways one can identify his/her claims--look at one's jobs, skills, experience, degrees, talents, certificates, passions, interests, hobbies, etc.--many benefit from using personality and work type tests. These tests aid one in knowing thyself. Three proven tests that have been helpful to me and others in my network are:

- o Myers Brigg--<u>http://www.myersbriggs.org/</u>
- o Strong Interest Inventory--<u>https://www.cpp.com/products/strong/index.aspx</u>
- o Performance Index--<u>http://www.rhsweeney.com/</u> (The distribution rights to this exam in Texas are owned by R.H. Sweeney. You can contact my friend Bob Panico at: <u>Bob@rhsweeney.com</u>)
- o Strengths Finder--<u>http://www.strengthsfinder.com/</u>

WHAT ARE THE CHARACTERISTICS OF YOUR BRAND STATEMENT?

You have completed your self-assessment. You have determined who you are and what you do best. You have chosen to stake out three-to-five claims. Now it is time to piece those claims together. It is time to package them into a brand. That is, it is time to create a brand statement. This step is arguably the most difficult part of branding yourself. That is because most people find it difficult to create a brand message that can be stated in less than twenty-five words! Your brand statement should possess the following five characteristics--1) Brevity, 2) Sounds Good to the Ear, 3) Authoritative, 4) Unique, and 5) Value Proposition.

1. Brevity

   Let's go back to our hypothetical marketer and look at her brand statement. We will dissect this brand statement to identify the key characteristics that every brand statement should possess. Her brand statement was, "I am a financially-savvy marketer who uses social media to drive customer advocacy." The first characteristic of this brand statement is its brevity. Her brand statement is not a stump speech. It is not a three-minute monologue. It states clearly and concisely who she is and what she does best. It packs a punch despite only being fourteen words in length. Much like a newspaper headline, every word is carefully chosen and no extraneous words are part of the brand statement.

   What do I mean?

   o She could have chosen to say, "I have an MBA in Finance and have experience in evaluating the profitability of advertising contracts..." While this is true, it does not pack the punch of claiming that she is "financially-savvy." When someone asks her to justify how she is "financially-savvy", the longer explanation will be needed and relevant.

   o Let's consider a second example. Instead of using the phrase "to drive customer advocacy", she could have said: "I spent three years at the CPG firm building a brand of snacks that saw repeat sales increase from 30 percent to 45 percent. But what was more exciting, was that 10 percent of all purchases resulted not from marketing efforts but from loyal customers who convinced their friends to try the snack!" While this is a great success story that shows she understands the difference between customer loyalty and customer advocacy, it would distract the hearer from clearly grasping her claim of customer advocacy. That is, the hearer can lose sight of the forest given the focus on the individual trees.

Do not underestimate the importance of the brevity of the brand statement. Your job is to convey who you are and what you do best in the fewest number of words possible. You do not want the hearer to navigate through a two minute explanation and be forced to determine what three-to-five claims you were making. You do not want the hearer to lose focus for ten seconds (glancing at their email, daydreaming, etc.) and miss one of your claims. You do not want them to be so intrigued about one of your embedded explanations that they go down a rabbit-trail and miss the holistic picture you are attempting to paint. Be clear. Be concise. Be brief. Just be willing to repeat your brand statement because they are so surprised you answered the question so quickly!

2. Sounds Good to the Ear
    The second characteristic of her brand statement--"I am a financially-savvy marketer who uses social media to drive customer advocacy"--is it sounds good to the hearing. The brand statement is not awkward. It is not difficult to recite. It is not difficult to remember. It does not have words that that are uncommon or hard to understand. It is pleasant sounding. It is easy to remember.

What do I mean? Let's consider how a simple, pleasant sounding brand statement could have sounded. What do you think of this second version? "I am a marketer, with an MBA in Finance, who is sagacious in dealing with marketing from a financial perspective. I am experienced in using websites like Facebook and LinkedIn. I have a proven track record in increasing sales via customer guidance." Do you think this is clearer? Do you think it states more accurately what she wants the listener to say? Do you think everybody understands every word she used?

The answer is no! The second version, while still rather short, is seriously flawed.

- o First, the first sentence has an embedded parenthetical clause that breaks up the sentence--"I am a marketer, *with an MBA in Finance*, who is..."
- o Second, while many know that sagacious means shrewd or savvy, many don't. Worse, some may even confuse it with salacious which means bawdy, carnal, or erotic (amongst others).
- o Third, stating you are "financially-savvy" is a much stronger claim than "dealing with marketing from a financial perspective."
- o Fourth, the mention of two social media websites is a much weaker claim than stating that you use "social media." It could cause the listener to think that you only have experience with those two websites which creates the possibility of you having one other obstacle to overcome in your conversation.
- o Fifth, the claim you have a proven track record in increasing sales limits the scope of your accomplishments. Did you also increase profits? Wouldn't it be better to say something ("drive customer advocacy") that is usually assumed to do both?
- o Finally, choosing to use the term "customer guidance" is much weaker than "customer advocacy." Yes, customer advocacy is one customer guiding another customer to purchase a product or service. It is just that "customer guidance" does not carry the marketing punch that "customer advocacy" does.

I hope this flawed version of a brand statement demonstrates how important it is for the brand statement to be pleasant sounding. A smooth brand statement, a brand statement without complicated words, and a brand statement without abrupt or awkward pauses will be much more memorable.

3. Authoritative
   The third characteristic of a good brand statement is it is authoritative. Being seen as an authority isn't just about acquiring a degree or accumulating up a set of experiences. It entails having a well-thought-out point-of-view. It is about knowing what you have that most others do not. It's your expertise. In every job and at every stage in your career, you had some expertise, some content that makes you

interesting. It gives you a cause, an idea, a trend, or a skill--the subject matter on which you are an (or the) authority. [Ferrazzi, p. 206] The key is to weave this sense of authority into your brand statement.

Let's go back to our hypothetical marketer and look at how her brand statement had authority.

o   Notice she does not state that she has an MBA in Finance (even though it can be used to substantiate one of her claims).
o   Notice she does not state that she possesses a laundry list of skills (the résumé is the place for such a list). Rather, she confidently and authoritatively states she is something. She is financially-savvy. She knows how to use social media for marketing purposes. She knows the difference between customer loyalty and customer advocacy. It is up to the listener to challenge those claims. It is up to her to defend those claims.

Another way of looking at an authoritative brand statement is to consider one that is not. For example, consider this brand statement for a potential controller candidate, "I am a strategic partner that focuses on operational results and accountability supported by metrics." At first glance, the brand statement appears to meet our standards. There is an authoritative claim to be a "strategic partner." But on second glance, the brand statement is rather weak. There is only one real claim--"strategic partner"--but even that claim doesn't really tell you much if anything about the candidate. There is a claim of authority that he uses metrics to validate operational results and accountability but that is so subtle it could be missed by many. So this second brand statement--in the end--is rather weak and bland. It lacks a confident, authoritative air.

4. Unique
    The fourth characteristic of a good brand statement is that it should be unique. Your brand statement involves finding out what's really in a name--your name. It calls for you to identify your uniqueness and

how you can put that uniqueness to work. It's not a specific task so much as the cultivation of a mind-set. [Ferrazzi, pp. 228-229]

To effectively influence people, you have to stand for something. You have to represent something. You have to be something. Your brand statement must have a distinct message. You want to stand out. You want to be the brown egg in a carton of white eggs! Gone are the days of being content to simply be a box of Cheerios on the cereal aisle and expect a sizeable number of people to randomly pick us out of a crowd. [Sinclair, *Branded: Sharing Jesus with a Consumer Culture*, p. 64] Gone are the days where your value as an employee was linked to your loyalty and seniority. Companies use branding to develop strong, enduring relationship with customers. Likewise, you must do the same with your brand statement.

When it comes to making an impression, differentiation is the name of the game. As Tom Peters says: "Be distinct or be extinct." [Ferrazzi, p. 226] Tim Sanders writes: "Former Coca-Cola CEO Robert Goizueta once said: 'In real estate, it's location, location, location. In business, it's differentiate, differentiate, differentiate.' This is the most important facet of building a brand." [Sanders, *Love is the Killer App: How to Win Business and Influence Friends*, pp. 37-38] To the extent you can differentiate yourself--your person, product, or service--you will be perceived as being useful, memorable, or valuable. "Whether it's Ivory soap, Coca-Cola, FoxNews, or Michael Jordan, build a brand that will distinguish yourself so that people will trust you, like you, value you, pursue you." [Sanders, p. 36]

If you don't build a differentiated brand, you risk being commoditized. You become just one of many un-differentiated accountants, HR managers, programmers, salespersons, technical leads, or account managers. Consider what we think about something being a commodity. If something is a commodity, we are willing to buy it from the lowest cost provider. Commodities are neither valued nor treasured. Commodities are viewed as both expendable and replaceable. Don't be a commodity!

If you are successful in creating a differentiated brand statement, if you are able to avoid being perceived as a commodity--borrowing from Tim Sanders' *Love is the Killer App*--you will have access to people's attention. Attention is one of the world's scarcest resources, and decision-maker attention is something companies are willing to spend billions of dollars to buy. [Sanders, p.46] When people know that handing over their attention is valuable, they do it. Differentiation gets you attention. Commodities get only time. The difference between having their time and their attention is the difference between ham and eggs. The chicken is involved, but the pig is committed. [Sanders, p. 48]

Let's look back at our hypothetical marketer and note how her brand statement is unique.

o   First, she claims to be a "financially-savvy" marketer. How many marketers have MBA's in Finance? How many marketers understand ROI?
o   Second, she claims to understand "social media." How many marketers can make that claim?
o   Finally, she claims to be able to deliver "customer advocacy." How many marketers truly can do that!?

It is easy to create a hypothetical brand statement that is unique. It is much more difficult to create a unique brand statement of a real person. How do you do it?

In most of my mentoring sessions, I find uniqueness in one of three arenas.

o   First, some truly possess unique attributes--a degree that no one else has (e.g., an HR executive with a law degree), a job experience that few have done (e.g., work for the government of Saudi Arabia for seven years), or a skill that few possess (e.g., fluency in Chinese). These unique attributes need to be highlighted.

o Second, I find uniqueness in one's hobbies. While it is not intuitively obvious how this plays into a brand statement, hobbies and private interests often explain why someone is more successful in some roles than others.

I was helping one candidate craft a brand statement. He claimed to be "innovative." When I asked for some examples of his innovativeness, he gave me rather lame examples. Finally, in frustration, he told me that he had been awarded three patents and built small airplanes that actually fly from scratch! Those examples proved his innovativeness much more than his first set of success stories. Using this proof of innovativeness, we then found smaller examples from his business career that showed his innovativeness and allowed us to introduce his hobbies as additional proof.

o Lastly, I always find uniqueness in the combination of skills and experiences. Fifteen-to-twenty years into one's career, virtually all people possess a set of skills/experiences that others have in isolation but not in combination. It is possible for many HR executives to possess hospital experience. It is possible for most in that universe to have MBA degrees. It is even possible for some in that universe to have global, international experience (notice the universe is shrinking). But how many of these also are fluent in Spanish! Uniqueness is almost always found in the combination of skills/experiences.

5. Value Proposition
The fifth characteristic of a good brand statement is that it is also a statement of your value proposition. To succeed in tomorrow's workplace, you need (as Tim Sanders says it) a "killer app." [Sanders, p. 11] To become a great brand, your brand must be seen as being relentlessly focused on delivering value.

What is value? I found Tim Sinclair's work on this question to be very helpful. "Expensive cars don't always look better, drive smoother, or last longer than cheaper ones. Identical cotton T-shirts aren't the same price at Banana Republic and at Big Lots. A cup of Colombian coffee doesn't ring up the same at the place that sells Frappuccino's and the place that sells fuel." [Sinclair, p. 34] Likewise, an experienced Oracle DBA doesn't look smarter, communicate better, or stay in a job longer than a less experienced Oracle DBA (sorry Oracle DBA's!). A controller who also happens to be an attorney does not command the same salary at a mid-market company as it would at a Fortune 500 company.

Why? It is because there are two components to value--a met need and a favorable perception. Or as Sinclair states: "Met Need (MN) + Favorable Perception (FP) = Value (V). If customers feel they need a product and they have a positive perception of that product, value is automatically created. That product becomes worth something (money, time, energy, etc.). Said another way, for an item to be worth buying, it must not only meet a specific need, but it must also be perceived positively by the potential buyer. And, the greater need or the perception, the greater the value." [Sinclair, 34]

Likewise, if employers feel they need a skillset and they have a positive perception of the skillset of the prospective employee, value is automatically created. The addition of that skillset will be seen to--for example--generate additional revenue, increase efficiency, and/or diminish risks. The addition of an experienced Oracle DBA can decrease DBA contractor expenses or increase database up-time or performance. The addition of a controller with a law degree can decrease outside legal costs or diminish the risk that a deduction runs afoul of federal tax legislation.

Tim Sinclair writes: "A valued product not only has to do a specific task, but it also has to do it in a way that people like. A janitor who smiles at people and whistles while he works is worth far more than the guy who never makes eye contact and grumbles the whole time. Coach purses, with their extra soft leather and high-quality latches, are much more valuable than identical-looking generics made with chintzy materials. The advertised innovation behind a Dyson vacuum warrants a higher price tag than the simplicity of the Sears brand. In short, a quality product isn't worth much if potential buyers don't think it is." [Sinclair, pp. 34-35]

Likewise, a marketing analyst who is genuinely friendly and makes everyone around her laugh is worth far more than the guy who is bland and prone to grumble. A call center supervisor who coaches his staff to be efficient and customer-service centric is much more valuable than one who focuses on metrics and drives her staff relentlessly.

When you create your brand statement, it should always be stated in terms of what you will do for others! Prospective employers are not interested (or at least most are not interested) in what you want to do. They are not interested in what you want to be. They are not interested in what title you desire. They want to know what you will do for them!

Let's go back to our hypothetical marketer. Her brand statement does not specify what industry she wants to work in. It does not state what she wants to be in five years. It does not request what title she wants. Yet, it tells prospective employers a lot about herself. And, more importantly, it tells prospective employers what she will do for them! She will implement marketing programs that make financial sense. She will enable the company to use social media to drive customer advocacy. She will bring value to the company!

What do you want people to think when they hear or read your name? What product or service do you best provide? What value do you consistently deliver? Remember, the choice isn't between delivering value or not. All of us deliver some value. The choice is between consistently delivering superior value or risking nothing and being certain of mediocrity. [Ferrazzi, p. 51]

HOW DO YOU MARKET YOUR BRAND STATEMENT?

Once you have crafted and packaged a concise, pleasant sounding, authoritative, differentiated, and value delivering brand statement--it is time to market that brand. How do you do that?

1. A Single Statement
   First, you need to settle on a single statement that encapsulates your brand. Don't get caught in the trap of having several brand statements. Most people are very talented. They are capable of making numerous claims. But most are not so talented as to warrant making multiple statements of value proposition. Even Geico Insurance--whether it is the Gecko, the cavemen, or the pig--uses a common tagline: "Fifteen

minutes could save you 15 percent or more on car insurance." Stick with a singular, strong brand statement in your personal marketing campaign.

2. A 30 Second Version

Second, you need to develop a thirty second version of a brand statement. This becomes your elevator speech! A thirty second version of your brand statement merely requires you to add detail and substance. For example, our hypothetical marketer could state: "I am a financially-savvy marketer who utilizes my MBA in Finance and my experience in analyzing and measuring advertising campaigns to implement marketing programs that consistently deliver positive returns on investment. I am a marketer who has over seven years of experience in creating social media marketing campaigns that increased revenues and drove profitability. I am a marketer with a proven track record of not only measurably increasing customer loyalty, but one who has demonstrated an ability to create customer advocates."

The key to your elevator speech is to maintain the trajectory of the brand statement. You do not want your elevator speech to muddle up your brand statement. You do not want it to paint a picture that leads one to view you differently from the one you crafted in your brand statement. You do not want it to include details that are inconsistent from your brand statement. Your elevator speech must be consistent with and a continuation of the marketing message and value proposition that your brand statement was built to convey. Good marketing campaigns strive to set forth a singular message. Make sure that your elevator speech does the same.

3. Your Résumé, LinkedIn Profile, etc.

Third, you need to incorporate this newly created, thirty-second speech into your: 1) résumé, 2) LinkedIn profile, and 3) biography (a biography is a valuable marketing tool since it allows you to have the ability to introduce yourself to others without having to give up your résumé). Incorporating your elevator speech into your résumé continues the strategy of having a singular marketing message. You do not have to slavishly follow--i.e., word for word--this advice. Just make sure that the résumé summary, LinkedIn profile, and biography are consistent with the brand statement you have created. Just remember to not use the pronoun "I"! (See Appendix #1)

4. Top-Half of the First Page of Your Résumé
    Fourth, you need to dedicate the top-half of the first page of your résumé to this brand statement and sample success stories that authenticate your brand statement. While there are numerous strategies for writing a résumé (see Appendix #1), you need to know that this is the most valuable space on your résumé. As such, use it wisely! Make sure every person knows who you are. Make sure every person who reviews your résumé clearly understands your brand statement. Make sure every person understands your value proposition. Make sure every person understands and believes you can assist them! Then you can document your past employment history, your awards, and your degrees. Give them your best shot first.

5. Blog Site, Web Site
    Fifth, you need to create and maintain a blog site (or even better, a web site) that serves as a marketing tool to clearly articulate your brand. Your brand statement has made several claims. Use your blog site/ web site to build on those claims. Post your thoughts. Demonstrate how you would solve a few problems. Share wise counsel. Reference experienced colleagues. Recommend sources on the subjects. Use these sites to substantiate and extend your brand statement.

    Many people struggle with this piece of the marketing strategy. That is because they are not good at writing and/or they do not like to write. While I am sympathetic with this challenge, I cannot emphasize the importance of being read enough. There are precious few ways to more effectively broadcast your brand statement than by writing and being read. It reaches a wider audience. It works twenty-four hours a day, seven days a week. It allows you to carefully word your thoughts.

It eliminates the stress of having to communicate in front of a live audience. It is simply very efficient!

6. Articles

    Sixth, you need to write articles for trade journals, magazines, and/or company newsletters. Before you shoot me (particularly those who hate writing so much), remember that you can re-purpose material written on your blog site/web site. Much of the material you publish on your blog site/web site is perfect for an article in a trade journal or magazine. In fact, many of the articles I have had published were straight from my blog site or were edited versions of what I published on my blog site. If your goal is to extend familiarity with your brand statement, make sure that you use any available means given to you to do so.

7. Speaking

    Finally, you need to get on seminar panels (or even better, on the seminar podium as a speaker). These venues enable you to set forth your brand statement and allow others to get to know you. As you will see in the next section on networking, broadcasting your brand enables you to be known and to assist others.

    It has been said that speaking in public is one of the greatest fears that people have. In fact, I know of people who would rather risk life and limb than to face an audience of real human beings (of any size). While this fact is often made light of, a successful business career demands that one have (at a minimum) average public speaking skills. And if one acquires above-average speaking skills, one can differentiate themselves from their peers. (See Appendix #5 for a quick primer on speaking.)

The bottom line when it comes to marketing your brand is this: you need to take advantage of every forum and medium to broadcast your brand.

WHAT ARE THE BENEFITS OF A BRAND STATEMENT?

You have crafted and packaged a concise, pleasant sounding, authoritative, differentiated, and value-packed brand statement. You have effectively marketed that brand by developing a single message, developed a related but expanded thirty-second version, and incorporated this expanded version into your résumé. Now it is time to sit back and evaluate the benefits that accrue to you when you successfully brand yourself.

1. You Find Yourself

    First, you find yourself. Your brand statement becomes a summary statement of who you are. It tells others what you do best. It states clearly what value you bring to an employer. It identifies your passions, skills, and interests. It captures your very DNA! Don't underestimate this benefit. Most people go through life never actually knowing who they are. And even if they do, they never figure out how to convey who they are to others.

2. You Become It

    Second, you actually become it! That is, you become the person that you claim to be. This is a subtle but very powerful experience that you will discover. Having spent hours (or days) determining who you are, what you do best, etc. causes one to boldly proclaim to others that this is "me!" And the more that you claim this brand, the more that you actually become this brand.

    When I finalized my brand statement, I found myself thinking of myself as being a transformational servant leader. This led me to name my blog site "Transformational Servant Leadership", to research and write on transformational servant leadership, and to describe myself as a transformational servant leader. The brand statement became nothing more than a description of who I am. This experience has been echoed by virtually every person that I have counseled, when they work through this branding process.

3. You Become More Confident

   Third, you become more confident. Since you know who you are, you also know who you are not. Instead of trying to become what the other person across the table from you wants you to become, you confidently project to that person who you are! You don't scramble around trying to remember which version of your résumé you sent to a potential future employer. You don't review your notes trying to remember what claims you made in a telephone interview. You don't roll up your other sleeve (think of a watch salesperson on the streets of Manhattan) and ask if you like a different watch than the one you showed on the other wrist!

   I remember in 2009 how this played out in real life. I was one of two finalists for a job in Missouri. They liked my résumé, they liked my first telephone interview, and they were very interested in a deeper dialogue to determine if I possessed the character and chemistry needed for the position. Twenty minutes into this discussion, I raised my hands and signaled "time-out!" I stated something like: "I am the wrong person for this position. You have a well-run organization and desire to turn it into a world-class organization. I fix broken things. I do not have the patience to move an organization from well-run to best-in-class. But I do know of a candidate or two who would be the perfect fit for the job." You should have seen the face of the hiring manager. I was unemployed. They liked me. They were interested in possibly hiring me. Yet, I said I was the wrong candidate.

   Why did I take myself out of consideration for this position? It was because I was confident. I knew what I did well and what I didn't do well. It made no sense to me to take a job and six months later be bored or frustrated. I love fixing broken and underperforming organizations. I don't love turning well-run organizations into world-class organizations. Knowing who I am deep down inside, allowed me to confidently state that I was the wrong person for the job.

4. You Influence the Direction and Nature of the Interview
    Fourth, you influence the direction and nature of the interview. Having clearly stated three-to-five claims (that are real, resonating, and relevant in your brand statement), don't be surprised when the subject of the interview immediately begins to focus on those claims. I call it the home field advantage!

    What do I mean? When our hypothetical marketer makes her claims of being "financially-savvy", being experienced in "social media", and knowing how to drive "customer advocacy"--since these claims are very relevant and meet needs that a future employer has--don't you think that the future employer will probe into these claims? "What do you mean that you are financially-savvy?" "How did you successfully use social media?" "How did you achieve customer advocacy?" And when they probe into your claims, you have a toolkit of success stories from which you draw upon (as is appropriate for the audience) to substantiate your claims.

    I hear some of you saying--"It doesn't always work that way!" You are correct. There are fact checkers, *&#holes, and control freaks who will not allow you to take control of the interview. Just remember these people are the exceptions. Most of those who you will interview with will happily listen to your claims and immediately open a dialogue about those claims. Why? Because they are relevant, they resonate, and they deliver value. All things important to the interviewer.

5. It is More than a Gimmick
    Finally, this strategy is more than a gimmick. Some will conclude this strategy over simplifies the branding process. They will argue for multiple résumés, various personas, and/or lengthier branding efforts. As stated earlier, the branding approach I am suggesting is not the only method or the best method. It is merely a proven method. As such, the beauty of this method is its simplicity. It allows you to create a statement of who you are and what value you bring to a future employer without the message being lost in the clutter. It allows you to have a single message. It allows you to be the person you claim to be. It is simple! If that is a gimmick, so be it!

SECTION

2 Connecting (Building Your Network)

Now that you have defined who you are, determined what makes you unique, and packaged that into a brand statement--that is, you have characterized yourself--it is time to connect with others. That was the second major lesson I learned in transition.

Mosquitoes refuse to bite him purely out of disdain. He has inside jokes with complete strangers. He once had an awkward moment, just to see what it was like. He once brought a smart phone to a counseling session, just to even the odds. He can speak Spanish in English. He has won the lifetime sales achievement award.....twice. His personality is so polarizing he is unable to carry credit cards. He once claimed to teach a German Shepard how to bark in Russian. He once ran a marathon just because it was on his way to a network coffee. Company Presidents take time off on his birthday. He's won trophies for his game face alone. Sharks have a week dedicated to him. He lives vicariously through himself. [Sal Bommarito, *22 of the Best Dos Equis "The Most Interesting Man in the World Quotes*]

> He is – the most disgusting person in the
> world! He is the networking jerk!

As Keith Ferrazi notes, every one of us knows him/her. He is the man or she is the woman with a smile on their face and business cards tucked into every pocket, notebook, and carrying case. They are always looking at others in the room. They join church Sunday school classes in order to sell insurance policies. They have a pre-rehearsed speech that is designed to disarm and disrobe (figuratively) every person they meet. "He or she is the insincere, ruthless, ambitious glad-hander you don't want to become." [Ferrazzi, p. 56]

The networking jerk is the image that many people have when they hear the word networking. But my view of networking differs immensely. "In my world, this breed of hyper-Rolodex-builder and card-counter fails to grasp the nuances of authentic connecting." [Ferrazzi, p. 56]

To better enable you to connect with others, I want to introduce you to a paradigm shift. Many have heard of the need to build a pay-it-forward network. Unfortunately, few tell you how to do it. Let me attempt to do so by answering five questions about connecting.

WHAT IS CONNECTING?

"'Gestapo! Gestapo!' The cry was urgent. The man was white with fear. It was 1938. Roman Turski, a Polish flyer, had developed engine trouble, and he had to land for repairs in Nazified Vienna. Next morning, as Turski stepped out of his hotel to buy souvenirs, this fellow slammed into him. Turski rushed him up to his own room, and arranged the man's slender body under the covers at the foot of his bed.

After the visiting Gestapo had checked his passport, they left without searching the room. The pilot used gestures to indicate that he could fly him to some meadow just over the Polish border. It was only after Turski landed in Warsaw that he learned the man was wanted because he was a Jew!

Turski later went on to serve in the Polish Air Force when Germany attacked Poland. After Poland's defeat he was sent to a concentration camp. Turski managed to escape and join the French Air Force. After France's fall, he went to England and fought in the Battle of Britain.

On one of his missions he crash-landed his Spitfire in England. His skull had been fractured and the chief surgeon at the hospital thought it useless to operate. But he awoke and saw a narrow face looking down on him. 'Remember me? You saved my life in Vienna.' Turski remembered and learned the rest of the story.

Before the war, the fugitive escaped to Scotland. He read of a Polish hero shooting down five enemy planes and crash-landing near a hospital. The piece indicated the flyer's condition seemed hopeless. He asked the RAF to fly him to the hospital named. Turski asked the man, 'Why?' The man answered: 'You see, I am a brain surgeon. I operated on you this morning." [Roman Turski, *The Evaders: Secrets and Spies: Behind-the-Scenes Stories of World War II*, pp. 149-151]

What is connecting? Connecting is "the process of sharing your knowledge and resources, time and energy, friends and associates, and empathy and compassion in a continual effort to provide value to others, while coincidentally increasing the value of your network." [Ferrazzi, p. 8] Let us de-construct this definition and notice a few salient points using this story as a backdrop.

1. It is Not About You
    As the story about Roman Turski shows, connecting is about risking loss. It is about making sacrifices. It is about placing the interests of others in front of yourself. It is about not expecting remuneration for your efforts. Simply put--it is not about you! It is about others!

2. It is Personal
    Secondly, connecting is not an impersonal effort. It really is about connecting with others. It requires that you give more than money (that is the easiest thing for many to give). It requires that you give of your time. It requires that you invest emotional energy. It involves hard work. It means finding ways to make other people more successful. It involves establishing a relationship with the individual whom you are helping. It may even mean risking your life!

3. It is about Giving Now and Receiving Later
   Thirdly, connecting is about being willing to not only give but receive help. It involves offering as well as receiving help. As the story shows, the time to ask for and receive help is not when you are helping others. The time to ask for and receive help is after you have repeatedly assisted others and have established a relationship. You pay-it-forward and reap the benefits at a later time.

   I will detail this thought later in the chapter, but your goal is to give now. That means you focus on helping, assisting, giving, and sharing. You build up a group of people who have received your gifts, who have benefitted from your assistance. You build up a network of individuals who are primed to give back.

   Now look at the second half of this equation. You not only give but you are willing to receive. Your network will be more than willing to give back because you have given first. One will merely have to ask for assistance once and the response of your network will likely be a tidal wave. In fact, your network will probably be pleading with you to help you--"What can I do for you?" "How can I help you?"

WHY DO YOU CONNECT?

1. We Should Place the Interests of Others In Front of Ourselves
   We should connect, first, because we should place the interests of others in front of ourselves. When the disciples asked Jesus -- "Teacher, which is the greatest commandment in the Law?"--Jesus did not hesitate. He replied: "Love the Lord your God with all your heart and with all your soul and with all your mind. This is the first and greatest commandment. And the second is like it: Love your neighbor as yourself" (*New American Standard Bible*, Matthew 22:36-39). We can go through life focused on ourselves. We can go through life expecting others to serve us. We can go through life never connecting. And if we do--it will be a very miserable and unfulfilling life. That is

because there always is greater joy in placing the interests of others in front of ourselves.

What do you mean? Networking jerks are focused on themselves. They are focused on benefits for themselves. They appear to be open to helping others but it is a façade. They are more concerned about leads, or contacts, or connections. They are not concerned about building relationships that may or may not benefit them. Authentic connectors are open to helping others. They are concerned about making other people more successful. They are concerned about building relationships that may or may not benefit them. They are concerned about placing the interest of others in front of themselves.

2. We Can't Get There Alone
    Keith Ferrazi tells of the story of when he caddied at the local country club for the homeowners and their children in the wealthy town next to his. "During those long stretches on the links, he watched how the people who had reached professional heights unknown to that of his father and mother helped each other. They found one another jobs, they invested time and money in one another's ideas, and they made sure their kids got help getting into the best schools, got the right internships, and ultimately got the best jobs." [Ferrazzi, p. 5]

    He learned that the most potent club the people he caddied for had in their bag was their web of friends and associates. "Poverty, he realized, wasn't only a lack of financial resources; it was isolation from the kind of people that could help you make more of yourself." [Ferrazzi, p. 5] This led him to conclude that: "the individual who knows the right people, for the right reason, and utilizes the power of these relationships, can become a member of the 'club,' whether he started out as a caddie or not." [Ferrazzi, p. 5] In effect, he realized: "it matters less how smart you are, how much innate talent you're born with, or even, most eye-opening to me, where you came from and how much you started out with. Sure all these are important, but they mean little if you don't understand one thing--you can't get there alone." [Ferrazzi, p. 5]

3. Relationships Are More Important in This Age
    Third, we live in an age where relationships are more important than
    seniority. I learned this first hand in 2002. In that year, I took an
    assignment that sent me to the Lehigh Valley in Pennsylvania. This
    valley had been the home to one of America's greatest 20th century
    companies--Bethlehem Steel. Unfortunately, for the Valley, Bethlehem
    Steel had been shutting operations down at its massive Bethlehem, PA
    facility beginning in 1995 and concluding in early 1998. This shutdown
    (and Bethlehem Steel's bankruptcy in 2001) meant that thousands of
    workers no longer had well-paid union jobs with excellent benefits.
    Even worse, many retirees found their benefits to be sharply reduced
    or completely eliminated. So much for seniority!

    What was amazing to me was how the Valley and the surrounding
    communities coped with the tragedy. Rather than becoming victims,
    the citizens rallied to support one another. Grandparents went back
    to work to replace lost retirement earnings. Children moved in with
    their parents. Churches distributed clothing to those in need. And so
    on. Even though I arrived nearly five years after the massive plant had
    closed, most had chosen to remain in the area and scratch out a living.
    "Where employees (like Bethlehem Steel) once found generosity and
    loyalty in the companies they worked for, today they must find them
    in a network of their own relationships." [Ferrazzi, p. 17] Likewise, we
    must amass a large network of relationships by feverishly connecting
    others.

    A common question that all pay-it-forward networking models stress
    is: "How can I help you?" It is a great question (though I suggest asking
    it in a way that is less blunt). My common answer to this question when
    posed to me is: "Please introduce me to other super-connectors." Why
    do I give this answer? It is because my network (however perceived)
    is not large enough to help everybody that I come into contact with.
    I have learned that one way to assist a larger number of people is to
    have a larger network to call upon. And there is immediate value to my
    network when others with large networks are interwoven into mine.

I liken this strategy to a snowball. Every time the snowball rolls over, it picks up more snow and gets larger. And by the time you get to the bottom of the hill, you have an avalanche. The larger and more diverse my network, the more people that I can call upon to assist others. The more that I can assist others, the larger the network of advocates, fans, or loyalists one has. And the larger the network of people who you assisted, the larger the network of favors that you can call upon--for others! [Ferrazzi, p. 16] The more people you help, the more help you'll have, and the more help you'll have helping others!

4. It is Like Exercising Muscles
    Fourth, connecting is like is exercising muscles--the more you work them, the stronger they become. [Ferrazzi, p. 19] In 2011, I shredded my medial meniscus in my left knee playing soccer. The injury was so definitive that the meniscus had to be removed. It could not be repaired. While the surgery was relatively minor (arthroscopic), I was shocked with how it affected by leg muscles.

The prescribed recovery program had me stay off my left knee for about a week with a gradual re-introduction of leg lifts, squats, and leg presses. Before I had even begun my rehabilitation exercises, I was horrified to see my left quadriceps had shrunken to about 50 percent of my right quadriceps! Having oversized quadriceps for someone of my height and build--it was rather noticeable and quite ugly! How did this happen? The muscles were not being worked!

Likewise, when we get caught up in focusing solely on our current job, meeting deadlines, racing off to soccer practice, pursuing hobbies, playing video games, taking our spouse on dates, raising children, and watching our favorite TV shows--we fail to invest in connecting. We fail to exercise our network. Failing to exercise our network causes our network to become limp and weak. We become less effective in helping others while assuring that our network will be of less value when it is needed for our own career advancement.

I found this out first hand in 2009 when I restructured myself out of a job. I had spent the previous nineteen years focused on myself--my job, my hobbies, my ministries, and my family. All of which are good things in and of themselves. I just did not focus on connecting with others. And as a result, I had a grand total of about 50 people I could call upon as being members of my network. Don't follow in my footsteps!

You should be constantly exercising your network. Like a farmer--who plants in the Spring, waters, weeds, and feeds in the Summer, and harvests in the Fall--we need to have a long-term view of connecting. We exercise our network now in order for it to be strong in the future. The idea isn't to find oneself another environment tomorrow--be it a new job or a new career--but to be constantly creating the community that enables you to find a new job (or a new career), no matter what may occur. [Ferrazzi, p. 44]

WHAT DO YOU SHARE WHEN CONNECTING?

Tim Sanders nails this answer in his wonderful book, *Love is the Killer App*. We are to share our knowledge, our network, and our compassion. [Sanders, p. 13] Let me provide you with some details around his answer.

1. Knowledge
    "By knowledge, I mean everything you have learned and everything you continue to learn. Knowledge represents all you have picked up while doing your job, and all you have taught yourself by reading every moment you can find the time. It means every piece of relevant data and information you can accumulate. You can find knowledge anywhere--through observation, experience, or conversation." [Sanders, pp. 13-14]

    We live in an age where information is more important than experience. In fact, information (or knowledge) is value currency. Someone talking about the latest reality television show may attract a brief audience at the coffee machine, but someone who tells people about Nicholas Carr's *the Big Switch* and who finds a way for them to connect the ideas to their careers so that they own the book (so that they can use it themselves to succeed in their jobs), is a person of genuine value. It's the difference between knowing which sports team is in first place and which new business idea can propel a career forward. [Sanders, pp. 67-68]

Power, today, comes from sharing information, not withholding it. [Ferrazzi, p. 146] "That is why you transmit knowledge. You're not just handing out some weight-loss hint or a workout tip or a recipe for a great tasting low-fat cake. You're giving someone knowledge that can advance a career. You want to become a theory-slinging, expert-quoting, knowledge-throwing person that makes you stand out from the pack and keeps them coming back!" [Sanders, p. 68]

Where do you obtain this knowledge?

o   First, you focus on books. They are complete meals. They contain hypotheses, data, research, and conclusions. [Sanders, p. 68]
o   Second, you need to be reading magazines. While they aren't necessarily intended to transfer entire thoughts, they can contain a kernel of an idea that prompt you to do further study. [Sanders, p. 68]
o   Third, you need to be perusing blogs for the same reason you read magazine articles--to grasp an idea that is worthy of further study.
o   Finally, you need to be attending seminars. These seminars enable you to hear thought leadership while interacting with peers. Bottom line: Share your knowledge!

2.   Network
     By network, I mean your entire web of relationships. [Sanders, p. 15] While we collect marbles, baseball cards, and antiques in order to hold on to them while they increase in value, the purpose of collecting contacts is to give them away--to match them with other contacts. [Sanders, p. 115]

Building your network works best when it's done with the underlying philosophy that every person is potentially relevant to you and your network. Sometimes people who may appear powerless or insignificant are potential network superstars.

This point was driven home to me about a year after I finished my in transition phase. I was aggressively building my network--and confessionally--by focusing on peers (other C-level contacts). At the behest of a friend, I met with an individual who was at the managerial level. The meeting was enjoyable and I set out to assist him in finding work. Low and behold, he began introducing me to people across the city whose networks dwarfed anything I thought possible. This simple manager knew more super-connectors than I did!

Building your network also works best when you include those outside of your industry and vertical role. Those in finance need to network with those in information technology. Those in marketing need to network with those in supply chain. Those in the oil & gas industry need to network with those in the healthcare industry. Those in manufacturing need to network with those in financial services. Why? Diverse connections within your network can accomplish almost anything. They can open doors for job seekers (including you). They can make it possible for you to be introduced to a contact (a person or a company) you did not have a direct relationship with. They can enable you to spin your web out further and further.

And, the bigger your network gets, the more attractive it becomes. The more attractive it becomes, the faster it grows. Real power comes from being indispensable. Indispensability comes from being seen as a connector--a person who makes introductions, a person who is able to parcel out as much information, contacts, and goodwill to as many people as possible. [Ferrazzi, p. 174] Bottom line: Share your network!

3. Compassion
    "By compassion, I mean that personal quality that machines can never possess--the human ability to reach out with warmth, whether through

eye contact, physical touch, or words. The beauty of compassion is that every one of us already possesses it. We are born with our arms reaching out to embrace. Unlike knowledge and networks, which we build over time, we all can tell people how much we care about them." [Sanders, pp17-18] Maybe you haven't read a book in fifteen years and you're daunted by the task because you fear it will take years to gain enough knowledge to be able to contribute. You may also think you won't be able to make enough connections to create your own personal network that will be of value to others. "But you can smile gently, slap others on the back, and shed a tear. You can hug, listen quietly, and say at a sad story's conclusion: 'I truly feel for you.'" [Sanders, p.18]

Why should you show compassion in your business endeavors? [Sanders, pp. 150-162]

o   First, there is a tremendous opportunity for your compassion to make a difference in the lives of others. Sometimes people need someone to touch them, to make them smile, to make them feel better about themselves.
o   Second, you create an experience that people remember. The ability to create an experience raises your value and drives your network. The truth is we are all marketing ourselves every day. Being likable is a large part of this personal marketing. Work is easier if people are drawn to you.
o   Third, you create an experience that distinguishes you. When you create an experience that distinguishes you, people remember you. When people remember you, your network grows quickly and exponentially.
o   Finally, sharing your compassion provides you with a larger margin of error during those times when you are less than perfect.

How do you show compassion? You make it clear right away that the focus of the conversation is for the benefit and happiness of the other person. You don't remind them of what they can do for you. Rather, you focus on what you might be able to do for them. You seek to listen rather than to be heard. You seek to understand rather than to be understood. You seek to learn what problems they are facing (i.e., what is your pain?) and you empathize with their pain. You seek to understand what they have committed to do for their boss. You seek to understand how you can make them a hero. You ask: "How can I help you?" rather than "How can you help me?" You ask simple questions like: "How are you?" The surest way to become special in the eyes of other people is to show them real, human compassion.

I believe that sharing compassion is one of the most underappreciated assets in business today. Every conversation you have is an opportunity to risk being seen as weak or vulnerable. You risk revealing the real you. What's the worst thing that can happen? They don't respond in kind. So what, they probably weren't worth knowing in the first place! Sharing compassion enables you to engender deep emotional bonds that both enrich and extend your network--for you and for those in your network. Bottom line: Share your compassion!

How does this approach work if you are in transition? Let me provide you with a suggested approach that has worked for me and many others. I want you to approach every network meeting as if you are a doctor and the other person is a patient. [Sanders, p. 102] Next, I want you to intentionally divide the network meeting into thirds.

In the first-third of the meeting, you play the role of the doctor (no doctor jokes allowed!). You ask questions like: "What keeps you awake at night?" "What challenges are you facing?" "What problems have you been unable to overcome?" The purpose is to determine their symptoms. The purpose is to identify their problems. The purpose is to identify how you can assist them.

In the second-third of the meeting, you prescribe the remedy. You share your knowledge--"I just read a book I think will help you, let me send you a copy." "I just read an article on that subject, could I send it to you in the mail?" "I just read a blog posting, I will forward the link later this afternoon." You share your network--"I just had a meeting with a CMO that faced the exact same challenge. Would you be open to meeting her for coffee or lunch?" "I know someone that found a vendor that enabled them to address that shortcoming." "I know someone that could speak to the hiring manager." You share your compassion--"I know exactly how you feel. Two years ago, I faced the identical challenge. Don't you hate how frustrating you get when...." "I truly feel for you." "I wish you did not have to work so many hours."

In the third-third of the meeting, you allow the other party to give back to you. Don't rollout a laundry list of requests. Do your homework (e.g., you know they are connected to an executive in a company you are interested in) and be prepared to ask only two or three requests. It is also helpful to ask for connections with others who might benefit from your assistance. Remember--connecting is about giving and receiving.

Why is this suggested approach so useful? Why is it so valuable? Why is it so practical? It makes your networking meeting memorable. The meeting is not about you. The meeting is about them. The meeting is not about getting. The meeting is about giving. The meeting is not about getting a lead. The meeting is about connecting. And when your meeting possesses these characteristics, the other party is much more likely (note I did not say guaranteed) to remember you. The other party is much more likely to be helpful. The other party is much more likely to share their knowledge, network, and compassion.

One day in 2009, I was across the table from an up and coming CIO of a $5 billion-plus corporation. He had somewhat reluctantly met with me as a courtesy to a friend. We were (or I had been) members of the DFW retail CIO community.

I followed the suggested approach I stated above. I asked a series of questions to find out what kept him awake at night. I then proceeded to share how my knowledge, network, and compassion could assist him in addressing his challenges and problems. About thirty minutes into the meeting, it dawned on him the meeting had not gone as he had intended. He actually enjoyed our time together! He and I were connecting!

While the meeting did not lead to him helping me find a job, it was memorable. It also resulted in a long-term relationship that has been both enjoyable and fruitful. We now willingly accept networking requests of each other. We now trade résumés. We are no longer just fellow CIO's. We are now friends. We are now connected!

This suggested approach (it is not the only or the best approach, it is just a proven approach) to a networking meeting has one other distinct advantage--it enables you to build a group of friends, advocates, and/or zealots. Imagine if you meet with and help ten people a week while in transition. That means in three months, you have over one-hundred sets of eyes to see things you cannot see. You have over one-hundred sets of ears to hear things you cannot hear.

For example, how many vendors or consultants show up on a Monday morning for a meeting only to find out that the person they were to meet left on the preceding Friday? They know of information that only a handful of others know. Like scouts, they are able to communicate these types of opportunities to those in their networks--before they become common knowledge. They saw something you didn't see. They heard something you didn't hear. And if they are in your network and they are your friend/advocate/zealot--voila! You know something before many. Which means--you can help others!

WHO DO YOU CONNECT WITH?

You connect with everybody. You include every former employee, vendor partner, consultant, friend, and neighbor. You include every person you meet at a seminar, every person who will connect with you via LinkedIn, and every peer that you serve with on a panel or governing body. Why so many people? It is because your network should include everybody that you have a relationship with. Remember--connecting is all about establishing relationships with others. Let's take a more in depth look at some of these groups....

1. Vendor and Consulting Partners
    To no one's surprise, I have found vendors and consulting partners to be my best networking contacts.

    o   First, they meet with more entities/companies in a week than a peer meets in three months. A fellow peer (be it a CEO, CFO, CIO, etc.) may meet with two or three entities/companies in a month. A typical vendor or consultant may meet with 10-15 entities/companies in a week.
    o   Second, vendors and consulting partners are always interested in you landing a new job at a company where they have a vested interest. They are even more interested in you landing a new job at a company where they have been unable to get their foot in the door. They scratch your back in hopes of you scratching theirs!
    o   Third, they love to help companies they represent who are in need of filling open positions. This makes them a great source of leads that you can assist them in filling from your network. That is, they are a great means for you expanding the number of people you can assist!
    o   Fourth, they host lunch-and-learns. These are great venues to meet other people. These are helpful in building up both your knowledge and your network. And best of all--when you are in transition--you have the time to actually attend these events!
        I commonly ask those in transition, "What is the common characteristic of those that attend lunch-and-learns?" They are employed! What better for one in transition to spend time with those who are employed (rather than unemployed)? It provides a perfect opportunity to share your knowledge, network, and compassion with a group of people who might actually know of real job opportunities.

2. Influential Individuals
    Most people assume influential people are the best people to network with. This is not true. The mere fact they are a CEO, CFO, CIO, SVP of HR, SVP of Marketing, or an owner of a company is much less important than whether they practice connecting. My experience has

been that influential individuals are often so busy they do not have time to exercise their networks. They may be very effective in assisting those in their inner circle but much less effective in assisting those in their wider network. On the other hand......

3. Super-Connectors [2]
   Super-connectors are those individuals who seem to know everybody and who everybody seems to know. [Ferrazzi, p. 128] Keith Ferrazi has a great explanation of how and why these individuals should be the cornerstones of your growing network. He writes:

"I believe friendships are the foundation for a truly powerful network. For most of us, cultivating a lengthy list of mere acquaintances on top of the effort devoted to your circle of friends is just too draining. The thought of being obligated to another hundred or so people--sending birthday cards, dinner invites, and all that stuff that we do for those close to us--seems outlandishly taxing. Only for some, it's not. These people are super-connectors. People like me who maintain contact with thousands of people. The key, however, is not only that we know thousands of people but that we know thousands of people in many different worlds, and we know them well enough to give them a call. Once you become friendly with a super-connector, you're only two degrees away from the thousands of different people we know." [Ferrazzi, 130]

In other words, it's not necessarily strong contacts, like family and close friends, that prove to be the most powerful. To the contrary, often the most important people in our network are those who are acquaintances. Why is that? Many of your closest friends and contacts go to the same parties, attend the same churches, generally do the same work, and exist in roughly the same world as you do. That's why they seldom know information that you don't already know. [Ferrazzi, p. 129]

Super connectors, on the other hand, generally occupy a very different world than you do. They're hanging out with thousands of different people, often in different worlds, with access to a whole inventory of knowledge and information unavailable to you and your close friends. [Ferrazzi, p. 129]

Where can super connectors be found? While some can be found in every imaginable profession, they do congregate in the following professions--executive recruiting, lobbyists, fundraising, public relations, politics, and journalism. It would be well worth your time to develop relationships with those in these professions--especially if they are super-connectors! [Ferrazzi, pp. 131-136]

4. Individuals Below Your Grade
    As stated earlier, adding individuals to your network works best when it's done with the under-lying philosophy that every person is potentially relevant to you and your network. One of the greatest mistakes in connecting is the belief that you only connect with those at or above your pay-grade. This is a huge mistake for several reasons.

    o   First, everybody has eyes and ears. If you are a Director in transition, can't a staff accountant know of an opening just as well as other Directors and those higher in the organization?
    o   Second, some of my most loyal network contacts are those who I helped find their first job out of college. Some of my most loyal network contacts are managers who I helped break into an organization that they had no relationships on the inside. These individuals, out of gratitude, often trumpet my laurels to the point they turn me into an urban legend! Don't underestimate the fervency and loyalty of those behind you in their career development. They are often quicker to assist you than those at or above your pay grade.

5. Peer Groups
    Throughout your career, it is very helpful for you to invest in a peer group. These groups enable you to ask questions and share experiences with others who are in the same stage of their career. These groups enable you to ask about and share knowledge about vendors and

consultants. These groups enable you to be heard and understood by others who understand your situation and your challenges. These groups enable you to empathize with others who are now facing problems you faced before. That is, these groups enable you to share your knowledge, network, and compassion while enabling others to share their knowledge, network, and compassion with you!

I saw this work first hand. A network contact needed an RFP template to replace their in-house data center with a managed data center provider. It was a smaller company that needed to move rather quickly. He asked for my assistance. Not having what he needed, I pinged one of my peer groups. Within hours, I was able to send him five (5) different templates--and as one fellow CIO mentioned--saved him several hundreds of thousands of dollars in consulting fees! This was made possible by being a member of a dynamic peer group.

6. In Transition

    If you find yourself in transition, it is valuable to connect with others in transition. I would strongly recommend joining a job support group. For example, www.CareerDFW.org lists all job support groups in the DFW area. The support that comes from sharing lessons learned (knowledge), contacts and leads (network), and encouraging one another (compassion) is invaluable. If you do not find yourself in transition, I encourage you to continue to connect with those that are. Not only do you benefit from helping others, you often get a jolt to your network. Why? It is because those in transition are meeting with and interfacing with hundreds of people. And often the people they are meeting with are individuals not yet a part of your network. Since those in transition are very grateful for the help they receive, they often ask how they can help you. It would be natural to ask them if they would facilitate an introduction to super-connectors not yet in your network. Remember, connecting is about giving and receiving!

7. Executive Recruiters

    One of the most common questions I get from those who are in transition and from those looking to make a career change is: "Should

I reach out to executive recruiters?" This is a loaded question. That is because my experience (and the experience of most that I know) with executive recruiters is mixed. Some prove to be very valuable while others prove to be less so. Why is this? While I cannot state with absolute certainty that the observations I am about to give are statistically correct (i.e., they are not based upon statistical studies using sufficient sample sizes), they are based upon my experience.

o   First, executive recruiters spend most of their time recruiting a position for which they have been retained or are hustling up the next retainer. If you happen to be a candidate or know of candidates for a position they are trying to fill--you are of value to them. If you are not, you are taking time away from the two tasks that occupy most of their time. That is, you are a distraction.

o   Second, not all executive recruiters are equal. Many are super-connectors. They actively work to assist those in transition even if they do not have retained searches that match those needing help. They freely share their network of acquaintances with hiring managers not yet under contract. They willingly show compassion to those who are struggling with making career decisions. Unfortunately, there are many who don't do any of these things. They are quick to return your calls when you can help them and slow to do so when you can't.

o   Third, many executive recruiters are transient. They jump from a large recruiting firm to a boutique recruiting firm. They jump from a boutique recruiting firm to their own recruiting firm. All along, they are under non-compete contracts that require them to be hustling up new business rather than helping those in transition. This transient characteristic often keeps them from being help-centric.

With that said, you should connect with executive recruiters. Just do so with your eyes wide open. And, more importantly, reach out to your network to find out who the good guys (and gals) are. Those executive recruiters are the ones you want in your network. And there are many in my network that I value tremendously (S.K., A.M., J.A., B.G., and E.G. amongst others).

8. Career Coaches/Personal Board of Directors
    Some individuals have been wise enough to surround themselves with a mentor. Others have engaged and employed a career coach. The most sophisticated have created a personal Board of Directors. If you have invested in these relationships, leverage them. These individuals can provide you with a wealth of contacts, at the right time, for the right reason. Why? They know where you have come from and where you are going. They know your strengths and your weaknesses. They know your aspirations and your fears. In other words, they know you!

One final comment about connecting (and who you connect with): connecting takes work. It involves a lot of sweat equity. It means setting aside 3-5 time slots a week to network (e.g., coffee, office appointment, breakfast, lunch, dinner). It means meeting with vendors (helping introduce them to others), consultants (helping introduce them to others), those in transition (helping them to find a job), executive recruiters (helping them to find candidates), peers (helping them to solve problems), etc. It means you have to think hard not only about yourself but about other people. Once you are committed to reaching out to others in an attempt to expand the number of your connections, you'll benefit from an ever-growing, vibrant network of people that you care for and who care for you.

WHAT ARE THE BENEFITS OF CONNECTING? [SANDERS, PP. 36-55]

Borrowing from Tim Sanders' work in *Love is the Killer App*, the benefits from actively building and exercising a network are numerous.

o   First, you build your brand. In the new economy, you are valued and rewarded for your knowledge and your network rather than your seniority or your pedigree. A successful brand will always give you powerful leverage. If you don't build a brand, you risk being commoditized. By becoming a knowledge guru, by sharing your vast network, and by being a compassionate partner, you create a differentiated brand that is useful, memorable, and personable. There are few ways to better market your brand than to be known for having a dynamic network or seen as a super-connector.

o   Second, you create an experience. When you represent knowledge, opportunity, selflessness, and compassion, you are not just a service provider or a product. You are fun, interesting, and valuable. You take people places they have never been before, you introduce them to people they never dreamed they would meet, and you show them concern and care that normally only come from family members.

o   Third, you gain access to people's attention. Attention is one of the world's scarcest resources. Attention is money. Attention is valuable. Connecting gets you attention. Others get only time. We are all multi-taskers today. All of us are busy. But when connectors deal with people, they can stop the multitasking and get undivided attention because their value proposition is high.

o   Fourth, you gain trust and respect. People will presume your arguments are correct, your recommendations are solid, and your referrals are valuable. They presume you have their interests at heart.

o   Fifth, you receive exceptional feedback. Because connectors give away their services, people are more inclined to tell you which of your ideas work and which didn't. They tell you which of your contacts were helpful and which weren't. The relationship endures. People keep talking to you. You learn what crashes, what craters, what flies, and what soars.

o   Finally, you gain personal satisfaction. As was stated numerous times in numerous ways earlier in the book, you benefit from serving others. Giving is truly more rewarding than receiving.

SECTION

3 Communicating (Protecting Your Network)

We have nearly come to the end of our journey. You have defined who you are, determined what makes you unique, and packaged that in a brand statement that tells others of your value to them. That is, you have characterized yourself.

You have also now built out a paradigm-shifting, pay-it-forward network. You have built out a network that is more about giving than receiving. It is a network that places the interests of others in front of yourself. It is a network that focuses on sharing your knowledge, network, and compassion. That is, you have connected with others. It is now time to learn about the third major lesson I learned in transition--protect your network.

Sherlock Holmes and Dr. Watson went on a camping trip. They set up their tent and fell asleep. Some hours later, Holmes woke his faithful friend up. "Watson, look up at the sky and tell me what you see." Watson replied, "I see millions of stars." "What does that tell you?" asked Holmes. Watson pondered for a minute. "Astronomically speaking, it tells me that there are millions of galaxies and potentially billions of planets. Astrologically, it tells me that Saturn is in Leo. Horologically, it appears to be approximately a quarter past three in the morning. Theologically, it's evident the Lord is all-powerful and we are small and insignificant. Meteorologically, it seems we will have a beautiful day tomorrow."

Then after a pause, Watson said: "Well, Holmes, what does it tell you?" Holmes was silent for a moment and then he said--"Watson, you imbecile, can't you see that someone has stolen our tent."

There is a danger, when we come to communicating with our network, that we look for the complicated and overlook the sublimely obvious. When it comes to relationship maintenance, we have to be on our game--24 hours a day, 7 days a week, 365 days a year! Simply put, we must protect our network.

In 2009, when I was in transition, I wrote a monthly email that was sent to members of my core network. These were the people who had genuinely expressed an interest in helping me, praying for me, and wanting to be kept informed. The email was never more than three short paragraphs.

The first paragraph was always upbeat--I thanked my core members for their support, I provided a short leadership quote, or I shared a funny one-liner. The second paragraph told the core members what I had been doing--the number of network meetings, the number of interviews, the number of events, etc. The third paragraph always reiterated, that despite my efforts and their assistance, I was still unemployed and in need of any further assistance they could provide.

It was amazing how effective this email proved to be. Those who had committed to helping me--but had not--magically remembered their commitment. Those who had not spoken to me in three months, requested that we get together for coffee again. Those who had actively assisted me re-doubled their efforts. The email did nothing more than ensure that I and my core network were in communication.

But it did not stop there! After I landed a job, I sent out an email on the regular date (I sent my email out on the 1st of every month). I told them of my new job, the challenges I faced, and my appreciation for their support. The response was overwhelming. I decided to send out another email one month later. My core network was simply eager for information. They wanted to be updated.

When the time came to send out the third email after landing a job, I surprised the core network with a newsletter. The newsletter provided both a business update and a personal update. It provided them with content from my blog site. It provided them with a calendar of speaking events.

It was a resounding success! Core member after core member told me that they appreciated being left in the loop. Most people drop off the face of the earth after they land a new job. The fact that I had not dropped out of sight, meant more to them than I imagined. Plus, my core members who happened to be vendor and consulting partners loved knowing where they might help me in the future!

To better help you understand how to protect your network, let me address six questions.

WHY DO YOU NEED TO PROTECT YOUR NETWORK?

While one might say that I stumbled into this valuable (but obvious) lesson, let me explain why it is so important to protect your network. The number one objective in protecting your network is to remember a simple rule: "Above all, never, ever disappear." [Ferrazzi, p. 94].

You have met individuals for coffee. You have left the office to meet others for lunch. You have skipped dinner at home to suffer through a steak dinner at a vendor-sponsored event for a group of your peers. You have met an executive recruiter for a round of drinks. You have taken an afternoon off to play in one of several dozen charity golf tournaments. You have taken up a vendor on an offer to attend a mid-week professional basketball game. In other words, you have spent a considerable amount of time and effort in building your network. Why would you now ignore it?

An Example of a Monthly Communication

First – How can I help you? Please let me know if I can be of any help to you or others you know. Can I assist in any way?

Where am I in my search for a new opportunity? I appreciate each of you for our relationships, whether new or long standing. I am truly blessed by your involvement in my life. Thank you for supporting, meeting, connecting, listening, and helping me as I go through the exciting journey I have been set upon. I already know that where I end up will be exciting and another challenge. It will have the potential to be of assistance to someone and some organization. The process is almost as exciting as the next challenge will be.

What is happening? I have networked with both individuals and groups attending 61 meetings and events. I have added 45 new connections on LinkedIn. I posted for 36 positions. I have been selected for eight interviews but have received no job offers.

How can you help? I am looking to meet people and companies that have the following needs: 1) They are challenged in some operational way and need an outside perspective, 2) they are rapidly growing and need someone to help take it to that next level, or 3) they need to deliver operational efficiencies and build performance into their team/company. If you know of people or companies who need these skill sets, I would appreciate a discussion with and a personal introduction to the person(s) you know.

The next report will be out the first week in mid - August. Thank you for everything!

The common failure of those who are employed is the failure to protect their network. They fail to invest, to share, and to exercise their network. Don't make that mistake!

WHAT DO YOU COMMUNICATE
TO YOUR NETWORK?

The elements of your communication are pretty commonsensical. The communication should always express gratitude. You want to thank them for being a part of your network. You want to thank them for building your network.

Secondly, you want to update them on what you are doing in your job. What are the challenges you are facing? What are the deadlines that are approaching? What are projects/initiatives that you are launching? This element of your communication provides members of your network with the opportunity to give back to you! It provides them with the opportunity to share their knowledge, network, and compassion with you.

Thirdly, you want to update them on items from your personal life. Did you or your wife just give birth to your first child? Did you just attend a ballet recital or a karate competition? Did one of your children graduate or get married? Making your communication personal is consistent with your goal of showing compassion. It is much easier to show compassion if you are seen as being a three-dimensional rather than a one-dimensional person. Plus, building a network of friends and colleagues is all about building relationships and friendships. Showing your personal side is a critical piece in accomplishing this objective.

Finally, you want to provide them with helpful material. As stated earlier, you want to provide them with content--book reviews, helpful articles, and/or blog postings. This is a significant part of keeping yourself in a learning mode, since you will be expected to communicate what you are learning.

HOW MUCH INFORMATION DO YOU PROVIDE TO YOUR NETWORK?

There is a need for balance in the amount of information you share provide to your network. Your communication should clearly address the elements just mentioned. But make sure that you are brief and to the point. Communications that require more than a couple of minutes to read are too long. You can always point your contact to longer articles but your primary communication should always be executive-summary like.

HOW OFTEN DO YOU COMMUNICATE WITH YOUR NETWORK?

The answer depends upon how you have organized your network. I have utilized a rather simplistic network structure. I divide my network contacts into one of three groups--personal contacts, core contacts, and LinkedIn contacts.

Personal contacts include family members, friends, and fellow church members. These individuals are kept up-to-date organically. We cross paths at church, at family events, via Facebook, and at soccer practice. There is no need to systematically update them on what is happening in my world since they typically hear about those events on nearly a daily and weekly basis.

Core contacts include those people who have asked to be a part of my core network. I have met with these people on numerous occasions. I have spoken with them on the phone. We have shared meals together. We have passed résumés back and forth. We have helped each other in solving problems. We have shared vendor and consultant insights. We share birthday greetings. In other words, the relationship is living and breathing. Those in my core network hear from me at least once a month. That can be done via an email, a phone call, or an in person visit. At a minimum, they receive my newsletter on a monthly basis.

LinkedIn contacts represent my weakest relationships. In that I am an open-networker, virtually anyone can be connected to me via LinkedIn. These contacts only hear from me when I update my profile, send a message to them, or answer a message sent from them. These contacts are aspirational. They do not get moved to my core network until they ask and/or we work together on some effort or event.

Obviously, it is possible for some contacts to be on one or more of the lists. The importance of having some type of organization is to guide you in how often you communicate to each member in your network.

Keith Ferrazi uses five categories to organize his network. [Ferrazzi, p. 183]

o   Under "personal", he includes good friends and social acquaintances. Since he is generally in contact with these people organically, he doesn't include them on a contact list.
o   "Customers" and "Prospects" are self-explanatory.
o   "Important Business Associates" is reserved for people he is actively involved with professionally. He is either doing business with them currently or hoping to do business with them.
o   "Aspirational Contacts" are a list of people that he'd like to get to know or has only met briefly.

Having now categorized his network, he then assigns one of three frequencies to each contact. [Ferrazzi, pp. 183-184]

o   "1's" get contacted at least once a month. He is actively involved with these individuals (whether it's a friend or a new business associate).
o   "2's" represent his touch base people. These are either casual acquaintances or people whom he already knows well. They get a quarterly contact (phone call, email, text).
o   "3's" are people he does not know well. They are merely acquaintances. He tries to reach this group at least once a year.

Whether you use my simplistic three-category system or a more complicated five-category system like Ferrazzi, remember this rule-- 80 percent of building and maintaining relationships is just staying in touch. [Ferrazzi, p. 181] Call it pinging or touching base--it is merely communicating with your network.

HOW DO YOU STAY IN COMMUNICATION WITH YOUR NETWORK?

Some people think building and maintaining a network requires twelve-hour days slogging through meetings, phone calls, email, and social networking. There is nothing farther from the truth. Building a network of friends and colleagues is nothing more than building relationships and friendships. It can be and should be fun.

Keep your business, social, and conference event calendars full. Work hard to remain visible and active among your living and breathing network of friends and relationships. Set a goal of meeting with 5-10 network contacts every week. Balance these out between vendors, consultants, peers, those seeking help in-transition, and your mentors.

I have found my monthly newsletter that updates my network on my schedule, accomplishments, challenges, and thoughts to be an effective means of communication. I have also found the newsletter to be an effective way of keeping my network aware of what I am doing while also sending out pleas for assistance (e.g., tell your network that you are getting ready to select a product or a provider and watch how many people raise their hands to help!).

Another way to communicate with your network is constantly looking to include others in whatever you are doing. If you are going to a vendor-sponsored event, offer to drive another member of your network to the same event. If you are playing in a charity golf tournament, ask a vendor partner to play with you. (Note: vendors like to get five hours of your time.) If you are meeting one member of your network for dinner, invite another member to join the two of you. (Note: you can always meet one thirty minutes before or thirty minutes after if you need one-on-one time.) It's good for them, good for you, and good for everyone to broaden their circle of friends.

How do you stay in communication with your network? Simply put, you integrate connecting with all aspects of your life which enables you to remain in the forefront of the minds of your network contacts.

WHAT TOOLS DO YOU USE TO STAY IN COMMUNICATION WITH YOUR NETWORK?

There are many excellent tools currently available on the market. You can maintain a core list of network contacts via Yahoo!, Gmail, or Outlook. You can leverage Plaxo, LinkedIn, or MailChimp. You can maintain a blog and/ or web site. Simply put: there are numerous tools and services that you can use to stay in communication with your network. With apologies to Tim Gunn, "Pick one and make it work!"

While maintaining your network, don't forget about important events-- anniversaries, birthdays, significant life events (the passing of a parent, the adoption of a child, etc.). While it is a lot of work, start now gathering that type of personal information. It enables you to distinguish yourself from others while ministering to your network.

In closing this section, the governing principle is repetition. Communicating with your network requires you to merely find a system that enables you to keep in contact with people regularly without putting too much strain on your already busy schedule. If you do, you will be rewarded with a living, breathing network that enables you to serve others while receiving from them.

EPILOGUE

2009 was a pivotal year in my career. Much of what you have read was learned in the six months that I spent in transition. It was a time of reflection, re-definition, and reward. At no time in my career, did I grow as much as I did that year.

How did it turn out? After spending the first two months spinning my wheels, I learned and applied the suggestions in this book in months three and four. The success of these suggestions was proven out in months five and six.

In those last two months, I made it to the list of finalists six times. Three times, the prospective companies did not believe that I was the best candidate. Three times, I was happy to receive an offer of employment. One of those happened to be close to home and proved to be the best company I have ever worked for. Thank you Safety-Kleen Systems, Inc.! The IT staff and business partners were amazing! Sometimes you are blessed beyond that which you deserve.

After joining Safety-Kleen, I continued to reach out to those in transition, those wanting to jumpstart their careers, and those wanting to enrich their careers. The lessons learned in 2009 and beyond have proven to be just as helpful or more helpful to others. While you are not guaranteed to achieve similar success, I trust that you will find these lessons practical and actionable.

One final note--As this book was being written, I found myself back in the job market (due to Safety-Kleen being acquired). That meant I got the opportunity to dust off these lessons and use them again in my search for the next challenge. Less than four months later, I started taking on the next opportunity to transform a broken and under-performing organization.

For His glory and His glory alone.

ABOUT THE AUTHOR

Mark Stone has over thirty years of experience in the business world. He currently is the System Chief Information Officer for the Texas A&M University System. He has been the Chief Information Officer of Safety-Kleen Systems, Inc. and Zale Corporation. While at Zale, he worked in IT, Financial Planning, Merchandise Planning, Database Marketing, and Distribution. Prior to working at Zale Corporation, Mark served as the Director of Financial Operations for the Resolution Trust Corporation and as a senior consultant for Andersen Consulting.

Mark is a CPA, an ordained pastor, and he holds a BBA in Accounting from Baylor University and a Masters in Divinity from Westminster Theological Seminary.

Mark lives in Bryan, TX with his wife of over thirty years, Deborah. He has six children and three grandchildren.

APPENDIX #1

RÉSUMÉS

There is no more hallowed subject, when looking for a job, than a résumé. The importance of this document causes people to fret over it, to re-write it repeatedly, to seek out multiple opinions, only to tear it up and start over! Stop! There are only three rules about résumés that you need to know:

1. Opinions about Résumés are Like Navels
    Opinions about résumés are like navels--everyone has one! There is no such thing as a perfect résumé. There are good résumés and bad résumés. There are proven résumés and unproven résumés. There are appropriate résumés and un-appropriate résumés. There is no such thing as the best résumé. As such, you need to develop a good, targeted, word-based résumé using a proven format that is appropriate for your experience. There is only a need to change the résumé if, after a period of time (30-60 days), you are not getting any activity in your job search. If you are seeing activity, leave the proven résumé alone!

2. Résumés are Overrated
    Much of the fretting about résumés originates from the belief that interviews are won and lost based upon the résumé. While there is some truth in this, if you are relying upon your résumé to get your foot in the door, you have failed to grasp the importance of networking.

No one looking for a job wants to lead with their résumé. Leading with your résumé means that you allow gatekeepers to grade/evaluate your potential value to the company. Your goal is always to by-pass the gatekeepers and jump to the group of finalists. When you do this, your résumé is merely a document that provides the interviewers with a summary of your history and accomplishments. And when your networking strategy enables you to by-pass the gatekeepers routinely, you begin to understand why résumés are overrated.

3. One Résumé Only
    This was spoken about earlier in the book. You have one brand statement and one résumé. The benefits of this strategy are numerous. You don't draft multiple résumés. You don't lose track of which résumé you sent to a particular company. And, you don't fret about whether the résumé is perfect. (Note: As stated earlier, if you are seeing no activity/traction with your current version of your résumé within 30-60 days, be willing to re-work your résumé. Seek out the counsel of a gifted résumé writer. Don't be a victim! Do something different!)

Now that we have established the ground rules for résumés (and now that we have de-mystified its importance), what is a good résumé look like? What is a proven format? What is appropriate for your current career level? While my opinion is just like others (see above), I would recommend that your résumé include the elements set forth in the following chart [Bonnie Dangel, *Resume Renovation*]. These elements were learned from my favorite résumé guru, Bonnie Dangel. Bonnie can be reached at: (www. bondanservices.com). To further help you, I have also included the three samples for those (like me) who are visually challenged! Do note how:

o   The formats are clean and professional looking.
o   The sections above the fold are given primacy because most résumés are only given 6 seconds of attention. [Huffington Post, *Résumé Design Eye Tracking Study*]
o   The résumés include an expanded brand statement.
o   Representative accomplishments are always stated in terms of dollars and percentages.

o The two-to-three page résumé is not a five page résumé in disguise (i.e., you are using a ridiculously small font).
o The résumés include your LinkedIn profile information immediately below your name (in a smaller font).
o The résumés are future-focused.
o The résumés avoid death by bullets.
o The résumés all have a skills section. Most job seekers think only IT professionals are fortunate enough to be able to list out their skills. The reality is that every single job seeker needs to dig deep and identify their core competency/skill sets.

Key Resume Elements	Sample A Project Manager – Business Operations	Sample B Buyer / Merchandising Specialist	Sample C Accounting / Business Analyst
GENERAL			
Reverse chronological resume style used instead of "Functional Style" (Functional Style is only appropriate for "C" levell executives)	Yes	Yes	Yes
Maximum length of resume: 2-3 pages (using correct size margins and proper font size)	2 Page Resume	2 Page Resume	2 Page Resume
Margins -- 1.0 inch margins left/right and .5 to 1.0 top/bottom	Yes	Yes	Yes
Reader-friendly font (TNR 12 or Arial 10) -- nothing smaller!	Yes	Yes	Yes
All post-college jobs shown, not just last 15 years but early jobs may be shown in separate section	1993 - Present (19 Years of Exp)	1992 - 2008 (16 Years of Exp)	1985 to Present (27 Years of Exp)
Entire resume is developed based on Job Target (future job interest). Thus, the resume is future-focused instead of being a historical "data dump" (all resume content written in support of Job Target (your next job!).	Yes	Yes	Yes
FIRST PAGE -- The first page must be written for a 6 second "scan" by reader			
Don't make 'em guess: Job Target (broad and specific at the same time) is used instead of outdated Objective Statement, giving prospective employer an idea of what you want to be considered for.	Yes	Yes	Yes
Branding Statement (aka Profile) is developed based on key words and is succinct in length, describing the "essence" of you (who you are, what is your DNA, what you do best, what value you bring to the party).	Yes	Yes	Yes
Heavy use of Key-Words instead of generic "universal" words, resulting in strong alignment between Job Target and resume content.	Yes	Yes	Yes
"You had me at hello" -- Page 1 functions as a mini "bio" creating high reader interest, with Pages 2-3 almost like an addendum.	Yes	Yes	Yes
Key Accomplishments and/or Technical Skills (Core Compertencies, Proficiencies, etc.) are identified with heavy use of key words specific to your industry/profession. Key words are NOT "generic" terms that apply universally like "team-oriented" or "highly motivated."	Yes	Yes	Yes
Key Accomplishments and/or Technical Skills placed at TOP of Page 1	Yes	Yes	Yes

Key Resume Elements	Sample A	Sample B	Sample C
	Project Manager -- Business Operations	Buyer / Merchandising Specialist	Accounting / Business Analyst
EMPLOYMENT HISTORY			
Employer line includes city/state and "primary dates."	Yes	Yes	Yes
"Primary dates" are flush right (not embedded elsewhere).	Yes	Yes	Yes
Company descriptor line added beneath each employer (to provide reader with context and scope of your employment).	Yes	Yes	Yes
"Secondary dates" (if multiple jobs within same company) are palced near to job title, not flush right).	Yes	Yes	Yes
BULLETS			
Bullets used instead of narrative paragraphs for quick scanning.	Yes	Yes	Yes
All bullets support your Job Target; otherwise, edited out	Yes	Yes	Yes
Bullets use the "Power Verb plus So What?" structure (begin with verb and end with explanation/clarification/results as to why item is important).	Yes	Yes	Yes
Bullets are results-oriented, quantitative statements (dollars, percentages, time, frequency, cost savings, size, scope, etc.).	Yes	Yes	Yes
In general, bullet list is longer for a recent job(s) covering a lengthy period of time than jobs earlier in career or if job was just 1-2 years' tenure.	Yes	Yes	Yes
Bullets may be organized under "sub-headings" (functional categories) to help break up long list of duties and to offer quick scanning by reader.	Yes	Yes	Yes
EDUCATION			
Degree earned (if applicable) with University name AND city/state. Year graduated not necessary, unless recent graduate.	Yes	Yes	Yes
Recent graduates should place Education at top of Page 1; all others should list at end of resume.	N/A	N/A	N/A
Recent graduates should list date of graduation, major, and include list of courses taken that are relevant to Job Target	N/A	N/A	N/A
Professional development, additional training, certifications, etc. may be added IF they are directly relevant to your Job Target	Yes	Yes	Yes
COMMUNITY ACTIVITIES			
Use this section to show leadership, high energy level, follow through/commitment, and/or "giving back" activities. Tailor the name of this section based upon your activities. Do not use outdated "Hobbies." Examples – Volunteer Involvement, Community Service, Awards and Community Activities, Leadership Interests, Presentations and Public Speaking, Memberships, etc.	Yes	Yes	Yes

JOHN GREENE

http://www.linkedin.com/in/xxxxxxxxx

4444 Denson Drive
Dunkirk, VA 22442

Mobile: 444.222.4224
johngreene@gmail.com

PROJECT MANAGER - BUSINESS OPERATIONS
Strategic Technology Solutions / Process Improvement / CRM & Sales Force Automation

Senior Project Manager / Director with extensive business operations experience leading cross-functional teams on Technology and Business Process Re-engineering (BPR) initiatives in Sales, Business Acceptance, Customer Service, Product Development and Marketing.

KEY ACCOMPLISHMENTS

Technical Business Solutions/Strategies: Recommended and led the development of a conversion to an automated process to connect client-facing web tool with back-office systems, driving a 340% service level improvement, with $3.2M in annual headcount savings.

CRM System Implementations: Led requirements definition for Siebel CRM systems upgrade including needs validation, systems testing, training delivery, post-implementation support and results measurement. Expanded Siebel rollout and achieved 100% Satisfaction Ratings.

Customer Service Operations: Won President's Award for developing call monitoring / coaching program to drive client satisfaction to 92% , representing a 9-point YOY increase.

Project Management: Led global product deployment programs; successfully managed deployment of Point-of-Sale (POS) application to 60,000 customers globally.

CORE COMPETENCIES

Process Improvement	Kaizen, Six Sigma (e.g. DMAIC, Affinity Diagrams, Cause & Effect Diagrams), measurement / reporting dashboards (KPIs), process mapping, Project Life Cycle Management, MS Project, MS Visio.
Systems Deployment	Business Case / ROI definition, budgeting, Statement of Work (scope & requirements definition), systems development methodologies (Agile, Waterfall, FISDM), UAT, Siebel CRM, Web applications, POS systems.
Sales / Customer Service Operations	P&L Management, budgeting, strategic planning, auditing, call monitoring and coaching programs, risk mitigation, cost reduction, training, problem / conflict resolution, Consultative Sales.
Management & Leadership	Cross-functional leadership, coach / mentor teams, strategy development, change management.

PROFESSIONAL EXPERIENCE

GENERAL INVESTMENTS, Dansk, VA   Jan 2008 - Jul 2012
A leading provider of investment management, retirement planning, and brokerage services.

Director, Business Analysis
Led cross-functional continuous improvement initiatives. Established and communicated project communication plans and created performance management scorecards (KPIs).
- Assessed processes and hand-offs from Sales, Legal, and Operations for effectiveness.
- Mapped operational processes to identify and target new cost/expense reduction initiatives. Introduced audit guidelines and eliminated write-offs associated with operational errors.
- Managed requirements definition for multiple systems projects, including needs validation and user acceptance testing, ensuring delivery of projected efficiencies/benefits.

DRONFIELD TELECOMMUNICATIONS, Dansk, VA   Apr 2003 – Dec 2008
A leading provider of distribution and technology solutions for the telecommunications industry.

Director, Sales Operations, 2004 – 2008
Managed strategic sales performance development, change and technology initiatives for the field sales organization focused on efficient product rollout, and market share growth
- Actively participated in the implementation of an offshore service delivery model, which delivered a $500M cost benefit.
- Analyzed margin, market share, and Win/Loss reports and developed resulting strategies to optimize industry leading share position.
- Led Sales Force Automation initiatives, including CRM (Siebel) and ROI applications aimed at enhancing sales force productivity and facilitating sales forecasting.

Director, Marketing, 2003 – 2004
- Designed and delivered targeted e-mail marketing strategies to enable new service delivery models, drive product adoption and enhance customer satisfaction.
- Facilitated migration to call centre based service model for 6,000 small business customers in Northeast while delivering headcount related cost savings.

EDUCATION / CERTIFICATIONS

B.S. Computer Science, Dabion University, Delkin, NC
Six Sigma Black Belt (in progress)

CANDICE BROWN

222 Danbury Drive   Duluth, WA 44224   444-222-2244   cb@gmail.comt

Buyer / Merchandising Specialist
Housewares / Gifts / Home Décor

10+ years experience purchasing diverse retail products including housewares, specialty gift items and hardware.   Excellent intuition with a "good eye" geared toward trend, quality and style. Fine-tuned organizational skills applied to managing multiple projects simultaneously.

Sales/Revenue Growth - Achieved a 13% increase in housewares category in Northwest with prior history of flat/decreasing sales revenue; exceeded corporate and store expectations.

Promotional Strategies – Planned and executed a seasonal promotional program by selecting an "out of the box" product mix of gift items to increase annual sales revenue during critical 4th quarter, resulting in increase sales of 10%-30%.

Merchandising Programs/Assortments – Researched vendor selections and selected a merchandise assortment of storage and organizational products for customer home solutions which yielded $1M in annual sales the first year.

Planning and Forecasting – Introduced a new feature to the forecasting system which allowed a team of 8 buyers to override the store managers' projections, leading to improved product availability, increased sales and higher customer satisfaction levels.

SKILLS/CAPABILITIES

Proficient in MS Word and Excel and purchasing/promotional software JDA and Connect 3 Other skills: strong math aptitude, keen problem-solving, and proven customer service savvy.

PROFESSIONAL EXPERIENCE

Kitchen Mix, Duluth, WA   **Jul. 2004 – Dec. 2012**
Specialty kitchen catalog company producing $2M customized catalogs for small retailers

Buyer - Kitchen Items and Appliances
- **Catalog Assortment/ Product Mix**
  - Formulated a balanced assortment of gourmet houseware product for the semi-annual catalog which reflected overall store images of client group.
  - Finalized pricing, discounts, terms, case packs, and stock numbers for 300 to 500 catalog selections with vendors for error free ordering.

- **Forecasting**
  - Calculated and communicated product projections to vendors to ensure on time delivery and adequate merchandise quantities to meet store's selling needs
  - Identified items that maximized promotional and marketing strategy that in turn bolstered annual sales.

Darvel Gifts, Duram, WA.   May 1995 – Sep. 2004
Largest gift store chain in northwest US with $100M annual sales revenue.

Corporate Housewares and Gift Buyer (5/95 - 9/04)

Housewares Buyer / Department Manager (3/92 - 5/95)

- **Revenue and Annual Sales**
  - Purchased houseware products producing $10M in annual sales for 78 metro retail stores; effectively translated customer and competitive information into action to drive growth and increased profitability.
  - Recommended development of turbo SKU setup screen to consolidate nine screens; saved two minutes per SKU and $2.4K worth of man-hours per year.
  - Increased bottom line revenue by $4K on a single, low cost/high volume item through cost comparison and negotiation of a reduced price.

- **Product Assortments/ Promotional Strategies**
  - Negotiated a customer-focused merchandise assortment with housewares vendors by analyzing costs, setting competitive pricing for assigned categories.
  - Partnered with Merchandise Planner to develop strong merchandising strategies, to showcase the selected merchandise mix, generating profitable sales.
  - Oversaw new store set ups including product selection; ordering and tracking of product for on-time delivery

- **Forecasting**
  - Calculated and communicated projections to vendors to guarantee on-time delivery and adequate merchandise quantities to meet store's selling needs
  - Monitored inventory levels and generated replenishment orders of continuing merchandise to maintain desired turnover.

- **Vendor Relations and Negotiations**
  - Sourced, and evaluated suppliers based upon reputation, quality, price, selection, service, support, availability, reliability, production and distribution.
  - Researched and monitored market trends and consumer habits to determine new buying opportunities.
  - Maintained strong vendor relationships and negotiated with housewares suppliers

- **Retail Store Experience**
  - Oversaw purchasing, reordering and maintenance of 4,000+ items generating $10M annual sales
  - Supervised and trained a staff of 7 employees in departmental operations.
  - Oversaw all facets of operation/merchandising and handled customer service issues, stocking inventory, cashiering and gift-wrapping.

EDUCATION AND PROFESSIONAL DEVELOPMENT

Some College: Completed 3 years - Donson University, Danbury, WA
Concentrations: Business Administration and Merchandising
Seminars: Negotiation Strategies / Multi-tasking Capabilities / Retail Operations

Mary Jones

maryjones@gmail.com

222 Danny Drive
Hurst, TX 76053

Home: (222) 222 - 5555
Cell: (888) 333 - 2222

BUSINESS ANALYST – BILLING SYSTEMS
Accounting Systems Analysis / Systems Testing / Sox Compliance Testing

---

Highly accomplished Business Analyst/Billing Systems professional with extensive experience managing Billing, Accounts Payable, Accounts Receivables, and Accounting/Process Improvement projects. In-depth knowledge of full-cycle accounts payable.accounting practices, procedures and internal controls. Possess solid understanding of System Development Life cycle (SDLC) in financial systems implementations to include systems testing and SOX integration. Fast learner with strong work ethic and high degree of enthusiasm for new challenges.

Technical Knowledge and Skills

ERP, Financial, and Billing Systems	Oracle/People Soft • Accounts Payable • General Ledger • QuikSet Manual Billing System (MBS) • Electronic Card Authorization (ECAS)
Accounting Functions	Billing, Accounts Receivable, General Ledger, Accounts Payable, And Revenue Reporting and Analysis
Applications	Windows, Data Warehouse, Decision Support System Paymentech Credit Card Processor, and Taxware
Testing Tools	Mercury Test Director, and Remedy
Office Software	MS Office (Word, Excel, Access, PowerPoint and Outlook)

Work Experience

Acme Accounting Services   **Sep 2005 – Dec 2012**
An emerging market leader in providing accounting and billing solutions and system integration services to large and mid-sized corporations

Accounts Payable Supervisor (Sep 2007 – Dec 2012)

Accounts Payable Full Cycle Process
• Processed the full cycle of accounts payable voucher payments: reconciled the open liabilities of $22M, re-issued payments, and audited employee expenses.
• Developed daily ad hoc reports for executive management on liabilities of $22M to provide critical current financial data for decision-making.

Testing/Data Integrity/SOX Compliance

- Tested system updates/patches and performed regression testing to meet Sox compliance standards and to ensure data integrity.
- Validated production data by running ad hoc queries, reporting errors in Remedy and making proper corrections in PeopleSoft as part of database clean-up.

Process Improvements

- Led a project team in the development of a Standard Operating Procedure (SOP) for the special handling of manual bank wires, reducing manpower by 10%.
- Developed a cost-cutting process to track Accounts Payable returned check mail which resulted in significant savings from reduced backend transaction costs.

Billing Analyst/System Administrator (Sep 2005 – Aug 2007)

Billing Auditing /Month End Close

- Captured accurate revenues by performing audits, developing daily ad hoc and monthly (Scoreboard) reports for decision-making purposes.
- Analyzed, reconciled and recorded monthly general ledger entries to balance the accounts receivables sub-ledger.

Test Procedures and SOX Compliance/Documentation

- Prepared structured system test plans, scenarios and performed user acceptance testing (UAT) utilizing Mercury Test Director for tracking and updates.
- Contributed billing expertise and business requirements for in-house project management system.

Business Processes/SOP Documentation

- Administered and integrated SOX (Sarbanes Oxley) requirements and quality controls with every business process impacting a billing invoice.
- Analyzed current policies/procedures and developed or updated Standard Operating procedures (SOP's) for billing processes to meet GAAP compliance.

Earlier Employment

Accounts Payable Specialist, Darvel Inc., Troy, MI   2003 – 2005
Accounting Services Analyst, Magnesson Corp., Troy, MI   2000 – 2002

Education

Bachelor of Business Studies - Management, Derby University, Detroit, MI
Accounting Emphasis

APPENDIX #2

BIO

While the résumé is not the mythically important document that most people have come to believe in, it does provide a level of detail that is greater than necessary for an introduction. Another vehicle for introducing yourself to others is a bio. Bio's are particularly good for senior-level candidates. A good bio should include the following elements:

o   A picture of yourself
o   Areas of expertise
o   Sample listing of positions held
o   Sample listing of professional experience and achievements
o   Education and certifications

Your goal is not to be exhaustive. This one page bio is to be an introduction. It is to be attractive. It is a vehicle for generating greater interest. It is a slick, professional tool that makes your résumé more valuable (versus the first document you provide to others).

To assist those who are visually challenged, let me share with an example of my bio that follows this suggested format.

Mark A. Stone

222-333-4444 (M) ◊ markastonetx@gmail.com

Transformational Executive -- Fortune 1000 Companies

Areas of Expertise

IT Strategy & Execution
Organizational Design & Restructuring
Process Improvement & Optimization
P & L Responsibility / Management
Mergers & Acquisitions
Budget Development and Management
Merchandise Planning
Financial Planning & Forecasting
Distribution, Supply Chain & Logistics
Real Estate
Oil Services & Refining
Business Continuity & Disaster Recovery
Security, Privacy, and SOX
HR, Benefits, & Payroll
Vendor & Contract Negotiations
Database Marketing
E-Commerce
Call Center Management
Board Relations

Selected Positions Held

Safety-Kleen Systems – Senior Vice President & CIO

Zale Corporation – Senior Vice President & CIO; Vice President – Planning & Analysis; Vice President – Merchandise Planning; Senior Director – Distribution; Senior Director – IT Applications; Director Store Systems; Director Project Management Office

Resolution Trust Corporation -- Director of Financial Operations; Manager of Asset Operations

Andersen Consulting – Consulting Senior

Education/Certifications

Certified Public Accountant
State of Texas

Master of Divinity
Westminster Theological Seminary

BBA – Accounting
Baylor University

Professional Experience and Achievements

IT Strategy & Execution

- Managed enterprise-wide concerns, including business processes and workflows, security and privacy, risk management, business continuity, compliance, as well as quality assurance
- Executed detailed tactical strategies that increased revenues, decreased expenses, and diminished risks

Process Improvement & Optimization

- Consolidated six accounting and operations sites reducing annual expenses by $8M, decreasing contractors from 1,400 to 600, while upgrading the talent and streamlining the processes
- Improved direct marketing campaigns driving $18M in incremental sales
- Decreased annual freight-out charges 35% while decreasing the number of days to replenish all stores from 3.5 days to 2.5
- Reduced the number of days to provide forecasted balance sheets, decreased the number of days to re-forecast brands, and increased the accuracy of margin forecasts and EPS estimates

Organization Design & Restructuring

- Implemented transformational plans that created order out of chaos, excellence out of mediocrity, and efficiency out of inefficiency
- Created a culture of cost-saving within the IT organization resulting in the identification of over $2M in annual savings in year one plus additional saves in every year thereafter
- Downsized IT staff 20% on two occasions, closed and moved a major distribution center, closed and moved a data center, and consolidated multiple accounting, operations, and processing sites

Team Building / Staff Management & Development

- Rebuilt teams on multiple occasions by stressing collaboration, stewardship, and empowerment to achieve stated corporate objectives
- Recruited key staff to implement a culture of operational excellence whereby effective teams owned the issues and their solutions

Mergers and Acquisitions

- Served on and led multiple due diligence teams in connection with proposed mergers and acquisitions of industry competitors

Vendor & Contract Negotiations

- Negotiated local and long distance telephone contracts reducing telecom expenses by $4M over a three year period
- Negotiated data storage that reduced costs $1.2M over three years while increasing capacity 50% on brand new technology
- Negotiated $40M contract to consolidate data and payment processing of asset management contractors

Security, Privacy & Disaster Recovery Planning

- Implemented disaster and business continuity plan and procedures for multi-billion national retailer
- Implemented policies and processes to ensure corporate and IT compliance with Sarbanes-Oxley, privacy, PCI, federal disclosure, and internal audit requirements

APPENDIX #3

PREPARING FOR INTERVIEWING

OVERVIEW

A job interview is the result of effective networking. Landing a job is typically the result of a successful interview. Many are capable of writing an effective résumé and making connections that result in an interview. Unfortunately, some hit a brick wall when it comes to offering meaningful responses during the actual interview.

What follows is not an exhaustive work on how to prepare for and conduct an interview. Rather, it is an addendum to the mountain of literature that has already been written on the subject. I wanted to share a few nuggets or pearls of wisdom that I learned in 2009 that were particularly helpful for me. I hope that they are as helpful for you!

BRAND STATEMENT

Be prepared to lead with your brand statement. While you are not in control of the interview process, it is helpful to rationally interject your brand statement into the discussion early in the interview. The primary reason is to answer that inevitable question--"What do you do best?", "What is your value proposition?", or "Why should I hire you?" The secondary reason is to guide the interview toward a discussion of your claims--the claims that define you, that project your value, and summarize what you do best.

If you have an effective brand statement, the claims will resonate and be relevant to the interviewer. It will be natural for the interviewer to explore these claims. Their interest in these claims provides you with a distinct advantage. It directs the discussion to those facts that are your strengths, distinctives, and value to the interviewer. In essence, you get a home field advantage.

Sure you will face that interviewer who wants to control the interview or the interviewer who wants to play mind games with you--be prepared. Work with him/her while navigating the interview back to your brand statement since this is the value that you bring to the future employer.

THE WENER QUESTIONS

I had the privilege of being coached by Steve Wener of Wyndham Mills. Steve has been in the executive search business for years. He invested hours with me preparing me for a position at a large Midwest retailer. Embedded within his advice was what I have come to call the Wener Questions. His coaching prompted me to make sure that I always ask the following four questions in each and every interview:

1. How much time do we have?
    He wanted me know at the outset, how much time had been set aside for the interview. This is a critical piece of information. In each and every interview, there is crucial information that you want to convey to the interviewer. If you think that you have thirty minutes (that is what the interview schedule says!) only to find out fifteen minutes into the interview that the interview is ending, you may have missed an opportunity to convey the information needed to make a strong impression. Find out how much time you have for each interview.

Work hard to figure out how to make sure that the information you want conveyed to the interviewer is conveyed.

2. What is the culture of the company?
    This question has two distinct purposes. First, it allows you to gather information that will enable you to choose the correct tone, the correct language, the correct body language, and/or the correct energy-level that needs to be used to quickly assimilate into the culture of the company.

    Second, it shows the interviewer that you are interested in learning about what makes the company tick. It has been said that many a person with the correct character and competency fails to be selected because they do not match the chemistry of the company. Here is a way to find out if you have the correct chemistry to fit in with the culture of the company.

3. What are the problems you face? What keeps you awake at night? What have you committed to do for your boss? How can I make you a hero? What is causing you pain?
    There are numerous ways to ask this question. Simply put, your goal is to learn how to tailor your answers (being honest of course) to address their problems. Your interview will be much more successful if you are speaking to matters that concern them. Your interview will be much more successful if the examples of your work successes mesh with their work challenges. Your interview will be much more successful if you speak their heart language. In essence, you want to say: "If I were in a position to address this matter, here are the preliminary steps that I would undertake to address this matter."

4. Now that you have interviewed me, how can my background and skills add value to _____?
    This is the greatest interview question that I have ever heard. How many times did you leave an interview wondering how the interview went? How many times did you wonder if your message was heard? This question aids greatly in answering those questions.

In preparation for the interview with the Chief Architect at the big Midwest retailer, Steve hammered me on the need to get this question in at the end of the interview. The Chief Architect was known to be a tough interviewer. True to form, he spent most of his time extoling his intelligence and accomplishments. He displayed an innate skepticism of my skill sets. He asked difficult questions. He asked open-ended questions. He asked trick questions.

Fortunately, I had been coached well and I navigated successfully through the minefield of that ninety-minute interview. How and what I answered is unimportant. What is important, is how this question enabled me to assess the interview. At the conclusion of the interview, I asked: "Now that you have interviewed me, how can my background and skills add value to _____?" For the next three minutes, he repeated almost verbatim all of the major strengths and claims that I had worked so diligently to communicate to him. He stated how I could address challenges facing him. He stated how I could bring value to the company. The interview had been a success! And more importantly, I knew that before the interview had even concluded!

That is why this question is sheer genius! Do you want to know how your interview went? Make sure that you ask this question at the conclusion of your interview. You will be amazed at how much insight you will gain.

STUDY THE COMPANY

While it is rather obvious, don't overlook the importance of learning about the company prior to your arrival at the interview. How can you convincingly show interest in a position that will take approximately 25 percent of the hours in your week with no or limited knowledge of the general job description, the company, its goals, or its current challenges? You can't. Here is how to understand the company with which you will be interviewing:

- o Get the company's annual report from its Web site (if available)
- o Visit its web site to read about the direction of the company and any current media coverage
- o Look over the <u>Standard and Poors Corporate Records</u>
- o Reach out to any and all network contacts who work for the company you are interviewing with

And for every company, you want the following information:

- o Services and/or products
- o Competition
- o Sales (and any explanation for a large increase or decrease)
- o New products/services
- o International operations
- o Any media information on the company in the last year

CONTROL OF THE INTERVIEW

Most interviewing coaches will tell you that it is impossible to take control of the interview. You are to act as the gracious guest and allow them to be the magnanimous host. Don't buy into this line or reasoning! Or at least, don't surrender control of the interview before you start!

Your goal for every interview should be to subtly wrestle control of the interview away from the interviewer. How can you do this? Let me provide you with three suggestions.

- o Use the Wener Questions
At the outset (preferably before you sit down), ask: "How much time do we have?" This allows you fairly wrest control away from the interviewer. Follow up as quickly as you can with: "What are the greatest problems that you are facing?" Most interviewers are very quick to answer this question providing you with precious information that you can utilize later in the interview (i.e., it enables you to pick the success story that will most resonate

with the interviewer). It also allows you to ask follow-up questions providing you with additional vital information.

o   Lead with the Brand Statement
This early statement of your value to the interviewer will normally direct the questioning to a set of real, relevant, and resonating claims that you are prepared to explain and support. That is, you guide the interviewer towards your strengths giving you a home field advantage.

o   Use the Jesus Technique
This suggestion is for those who have advanced interviewing skills. Often when the Pharisees challenged Jesus, Jesus responded to their question with a question. Once the chief priests and the elders of the people asked: "'By what authority are you doing these things, and who gave You this authority?' Jesus answered: 'The baptism of John was from what source, from heaven or from men?'" (*New American Standard Bible*, Matt. 21:23-25) The purpose of using this technique is to disarm particularly aggressive or hostile questions. It not only buys time but it often forces the interviewer to explain what they are really probing for. Thus, you somewhat regain control of the interview. Be willing to ask a question when asked a question!

One last question on taking control of the interview--Is there a metric to measure how effective you have been subtly taking control of the interview? The metric I use for my interviews is the percentage of time the interviewer is speaking and the percentage of time I am speaking. Don't laugh--my goal is to speak only 30 percent of the time in the interview! I want to gather as much information as I can from the interviewer-- the culture of the company, the challenges the company faces, the characteristics of the person they are looking for to fill the open position, etc. This ensures that I am then able to craft responses to questions in a manner that addresses their needs, wants, and challenges. I detest shooting in the dark! And, remember, you are interviewing them just as much as they are interviewing you.

Be careful! This metric is merely a suggestion. It is merely a guideline. You need to make sure that you allow sufficient time to state your case. If the interviewer drones on too long, there will be insufficient time to state your case. I have found that a clear, concise, value-laced presentation can be made utilizing only 30 percent of the time. Try this technique! You may be surprised to find out how effective it is.

PREPARE ANSWERS TO EXPECTED QUESTIONS

It's incredibly hard to land an interview these days, so making the most of every opportunity is critical. Many job seekers hit a brick wall when it comes to offering meaningful responses during the interview. You must be careful not to put your foot in your mouth when answering open-ended questions. "Tell me about yourself," is not the cue to begin your life story. Simultaneously, you do not want to blurt out an answer to a question so quickly that it is obvious that you memorized the answer!

Interviewing is like being selected to compete in the Olympics--you have outperformed hundreds or thousands of competitors and are down to the final round. You are now competing with the best of the best. How can you leave with the gold? One of the most important things that you can do is to have prepared, not memorized answers to typical interview questions.

To assist you in this process, I am going to provide you with possible answers to two groups of interview questions:

o   The most common questions, and
o   Other typical interview questions

Recently, RésuméDoctor.com surveyed over 2,000 recruiters and hiring managers worldwide in order to find out what questions are most frequently asked during job interviews. [Resume Doctor, *Top Questions Asked at Job Interviews*.] Participants came from a variety of industries, including information technology, marketing and sales, finance, and healthcare. The top 15 interview questions, in descending order, are:

1. Describe your ideal job and/or boss.
    Be generic and positive. Safe qualities are knowledgeable, a sense of humor, fair, loyal to subordinates, and holder of high standards. All bosses like to think they have these traits.

2. Why are you looking for a job? Why are leaving your current position? Stay positive regardless of the circumstances. Never refer to a major problem with management and never speak ill of supervisors, co-workers, or the organization. If you do, you will be the one looking bad. Keep smiling and talk about leaving for a positive reason such as an opportunity, a chance to do something special, or other forward-looking reasons.

3. What unique experience or qualifications separate you from other candidates?
    This is the perfect time to highlight your primary claims in your branding statement--particularly those that differentiate yourself. Recognize also, that sometimes your differentiation is that you possess a combination of skills. You possess skills that are often found singularly in others but are found in combination with yourself.

4. Tell me about yourself.
    This is the perfect time to use your thirty-second elevator speech, which of course, is an expanded version of your brand statement.

5. What are your strengths and weaknesses?
    The first part of this question is easy--if you have developed your brand statement. The answer to the question of what is your greatest strength is your brand statement. The answer to the question of what is your greatest weakness, is a completely different matter. Many seekers think this is a trick question, designed to make you confess the reason why you shouldn't be hired. This leads to the common tactic of trying to turn a negative into a positive. "I am intolerant of incompetence." Or, "I become so focused that I find myself working evenings and weekends."

While this tactic looks good on the surface, most interviewers are so experienced that they dislike this approach. A better approach is to show that you know yourself and are committed to personal development. A better answer might sound something like: "I'm committed to my own personal development, and every year I focus on two or three skill areas that I know need improvement. This year I wanted to beef up my negotiating skills. So, I've taken attended a seminar on negotiating and have read three books on the topic."

6. Describe some of your most important career accomplishments.
    If you have done your homework, if you have asked pertinent questions in the early part of the interview, this is a softball question. Look into your toolbox of success stories and select those stories that would be the most relevant to the challenges the interviewer and the company are facing.

7. What are your short-term/long-term goals?
    Be careful, this can be a trap question. Some interviewers are merely trying to determine if your expectations match the opportunity for which you are interviewing for. That is, they are trying to determine if you will be content or frustrated in this role and in the career path in which it sits. Be honest! There is no job worth taking if you will be frustrated with the future opportunity for upward mobility or the pressure to advance faster than your lifestyle will allow.

8. Describe a time when you were faced with a challenging situation and how you handled it.
    Pick a specific incident. Concentrate on your problem solving technique and not the dispute you settled.

9. What are your salary requirements?
    The overall strategy is to delay stating a specific salary number until the company has decided to hire you. Any discussion of compensation before this time runs a high risk of eliminating you from further consideration. Your strategy should be to state:

o   I was paid well and in line with job market conditions.
o   You'd be happy to discuss salary history later in the hiring process.
o   You're interested in the opportunity so far.

For example:

o   "I desire for a compensation package that is commensurate with the position we are discussing."
o   "I was paid well in my last position and in-line with market conditions and the results I delivered. I will be happy to discuss my compensation history in detail when we have decided that I'm the right person for this position."

If they ask again, state:

o   "I realize that you need to make certain that my salary expectations are consistent with the salary range. To ensure we are aligned, please tell me the salary range and I'll let you know how my salary matches the range." Or
o   "When deciding on a position I consider the following factors; the quality of the opportunity, the quality of the company and the people I'd be working with, the long-term growth potential, the location, and the compensation. I remain very interested."

Remember that the first person to give a number is at a disadvantage. You want to discuss salary only when they are absolutely convinced they can't live without you. It is at this point that you have negotiating leverage and not until then. Craft a response that feels comfortable for you and practice saying it. Decide right now that you are not going to discuss salary until you are ready.

10. Why are you interested in this position? Our company?
    This should be based on the research you have done on the open position and the organization. Sincerity is extremely important here and will easily be sensed. Relate it to your long-term career goals.

11. What would your former boss/colleagues say about you?
    This is a rather easy question. Consider your most recent reviews/appraisals and select the two strongest qualities/capabilities mentioned by your boss--loyalty, energy, positive attitude, leadership, team player, initiative, patience, creativity, problem solver, etc/--and ones that would be of greatest interest to the interviewer (in light of your own research and questioning).

    When answering the question what would your former colleagues say about you, be prepared with a quote or two from co-workers. Either a specific statement or a paraphrase will work.

12. What are the best and worst aspects of your previous job?
    Make sure that you choose aspects that you love from your previous job that mimic the culture of the company that you are interviewing with. When addressing aspects that you didn't like at your previous job, don't get trivial or negative. Focus on safe responses such as: "I did not have enough of a challenge," "The company was not in a growth mode," or "There were few opportunities for advancement or personal development."

13. What do you know about our company?
    This question is one reason to do some research on the organization before the interview. Find out where they have been and where they are going. Find out the current issues and the major players.

14. What motivates you? How do you motivate others?
    This is a personal trait that only you can say, but good examples are: challenge, achievement, team success, or excellence. In addressing how you motivate others, make sure that you define your management/leadership style and provide them with one or two specific examples.

15. Are you willing to relocate?
    The answer is always yes! What do you mean? You can always say "no" to an out-of-town job offer. But you cannot say "yes" to a too-good-to-turn-down out-of-town job offer unless you were open to relocating.

There is a price that would cause every one of us to relocate (even though the bar may be ridiculously high).

Obviously, there are a million other questions that might come up in an interview. Borrowing a handful of questions from Wayne D. Ford's book, *The Accelerated Job Search*, here are a few other questions you might want to be prepared to answer: [Wayne D. Ford, *The Accelerated Job Search*, pp. 195-211]

1. Do you consider yourself successful?
   You should always answer yes and briefly explain why. A good explanation is that you have set goals, you have met some, and are on track to achieve the others.

2. What have you done to improve your knowledge in the last year?
   Try to include improvement activities that relate to the job. A wide variety of activities can be mentioned as positive self-improvement. Have some good ones handy to mention.

3. Do you know anyone who works for us?
   Be aware of the policy on relatives working for the organization. This can affect your answer even though they asked about friends not relatives. Be careful to mention a friend only if they are well thought of.

4. Are you a team player?
   You are, of course, a team player. Be sure to have examples ready. Specifics that show you often perform for the good of the team rather than for yourself are good evidence of your team attitude. Do not brag. State it in a matter-of-fact tone. This is a key point.

5. How long would you expect to work for us if hired?
   Specifics here are not good. Something like this should work: "I'd like it to be a long time. Or as long as we both feel I'm doing a good job."

6. Tell me about a suggestion you have made.
    Have a good one ready. Be sure and use a suggestion that was accepted and was then considered successful. One related to the type of work applied for is a real plus.

7. What irritates you about co-workers?
    This is a trap question. Think real hard but fail to come up with anything that irritates you. A short statement that you seem to get along with folks is great.

8. Tell me about your dream job.
    Stay away from a specific job. You cannot win. If you say the job you are contending for is it, you strain credibility. If you say another job is it, you plant the suspicion that you will be dissatisfied with this position if hired. The best is to stay generic and say something like: "A job where I love the work, like the people, can contribute, and can't wait to get to work."

9. What kind of person would you refuse to work with?
    Do not be trivial. It would take disloyalty to the organization, violence or law-breaking to get you to object. Minor objections will label you as a whiner.

10. What is more important to you, the money or the work?
    Money is always important, but the work is the most important. There is no better answer.

11. Tell me about a problem you had with a supervisor.
    This is the biggest trap of all. This is a test to see if you will speak ill of your boss. If you fall for it and tell about a problem with a former boss, you may well blow the interview right there. Stay positive and develop a poor memory about any trouble with a supervisor.

12. Tell me about your ability to work under pressure.
    You may say that you thrive under certain types of pressure. Give an example that relates to the type of position applied for.

13. How would you know you were successful on this job?
Any of the following would work: 1) You set high standards for yourself and meet them. 2) Your outcomes are a success. 3) Your boss tells you that you are successful.

14. Are you willing to put the interests of the organization ahead of your own?
This is a straight loyalty and dedication question. Do not worry about the deep ethical and philosophical implications. Just say yes.

15. What have you learned from mistakes on the job?
Here you have to come up with something or you strain credibility. Make it a small, well intentioned mistake with a positive lesson learned. An example would be working too far ahead of colleagues on a project and thus throwing coordination off.

16. Do you have any blind spots?
This is a trick question. If you know about blind spots, they are no longer blind spots. Do not reveal any personal areas of concern here. Let them do their own discovery on your bad points. Do not hand it to them.

17. If you were hiring a person for this job, what would you look for?
Be careful to mention traits that are needed and that you have.

18. What has been your biggest professional disappointment?
Be sure that you refer to something that was beyond your control. Show acceptance and no negative feelings.

19. Do you have any questions for me?
Always have some questions prepared. Questions prepared where you will be an asset to the organization are good. For example: "How soon will I be able to be productive?" Or, "What type of projects will I be able to assist on?"

20. Where do you want to be in five years?
"I am looking for a position where I can continue to _____ with increasing responsibility."

QUESTIONS YOU SHOULD ASK

Prepare questions in several categories and ask them early--and throughout--the interview. That way, you will find out valuable information as you go. You will be able to tailor your responses and illustrate examples that fit the job.

o   Questions About the Job

- How would you define success in this position after six months? (You may hit a hot button that will give you more free information that you can use to sell yourself.)
- What are the most important skills and abilities that a person would need in this job to be successful? (If you possess any of these skills, be ready with examples to prove it.)
- What is the toughest challenge in this position, in your opinion? (Listen closely for the downsides. If you have strengths that will overcome these obstacles, be ready to illustrate how you've used them to your advantage in the past.)
- What happened to the person who had this job before? (If the person was promoted or fired, ask why.)

o   Questions About the Company

- I see that you have recently merged with ACME. How will this affect your department?
- I noticed that the company sells widgets in South America. I speak Spanish. Would that be something that I could use in this job? (Ask questions that position you to sell yourself.)
- How would you describe your corporate culture?

o   Questions About the Manager and Co-Workers

- How would you describe your management style?
- What are your pet peeves?

- How would you describe the co-workers this position would work with? Did anyone on the team apply for the job? Are there any problems on the team?

o Questions About Internal/External Customers

- Which departments will this position have the most interaction with?
- Are there any issues between departments that you would like this position to work on?
- (If you are a final candidate) Will I have an opportunity to talk with someone who does this job/or someone with whom this position interacts?

PANEL INTERVIEW TIPS

The panel interview can occur in any industry, and the number of interviewers can range from two to eight (or more). In order to succeed, follow the tips below:

o Panel interview technique # 1: Eye contact
Not knowing where to look during a panel interview is a concern for many. As a general rule, you should start answering questions while making eye contact with the person who asked the question. Then you should look around to the other interviewers and finish answering the question while making contact with the person who asked the question.

o Panel interview technique # 2: Ask Questions
Determine the leader of the group, and direct questions to her/him at the end of the interview. The leader is usually the person who makes the initial introductions and/or asks the most questions during the interview. For specific questions that only a person in a specific department can answer, ask the individual representing the department.

o   Panel interview technique # 3: Remain Focused
    The good/bad cop scenario occurs when one interviewer is friendly
    and another is harsh. This method is used to determine how you
    will react in stressful situations. Keep your cool, and do not let the
    interview to get under your skin.

o   Panel interview technique # 4: Respect Silence
    Do not feel the need to fill every empty space. Silence is a strategy
    interviewers may use to get you to reveal information you ordinarily
    would not. Avoid falling into the trap. When you finish answering a
    question, stop talking.

o   Panel interview technique # 5: Follow-up Letters
    Send a thank you letter to every interviewer. The focus of each letter
    will differ depending on the job title of the interviewer. For example,
    the supervisor of your department will be interested in your teamwork
    and productivity skills, while a member of a partnering department
    will be interested in your ability to work collaboratively with his/her
    respective Division. To ensure you get the spelling of everyone's name
    and email right, ask for everyone's business card.

APPENDIX #4

COLLEGE STUDENTS

INTRODUCTION

The rules of the game have changed. 60 percent of all college graduates are unable to find employment in their field of study [James Marshall Crotty, *60% of College Grads Can't Find Work in Their Field. Is a Management Degree the Answer?*] While we could debate how much of this problem is due to college students getting the wrong degree, the fact is that college graduates are finding the job market to be more hostile than ever. What does that mean for you? How are you going to find a job in this new marketplace? What are you going to do to survive in this new economic order? What can you do in the four years that you are in college to increase the likelihood of finding employment in your chosen field of study? While I do not have the complete answers to these questions, I would like to provide you with a primer on how to plan, build, and enhance your future career--using the material in this book--<u>while you are in college</u>.

ASSUMPTIONS

The plan of action--**branding, networking, and marketing**--is based on several assumptions.

- o First, it involves a significant amount of work. There is a Chinese proverb that states: "A journey of a thousand miles begins with a single step."
- o Second, some of you will choose to be a college student rather than a young adult.
- o Finally, this primer is not a guarantee. It merely sets forth a set of wise principles that more often than not, yield success. I am mindful of what James writes in his epistle: "Come now, you who say, 'Today or tomorrow, we shall go to such and such a city, and spend a year there and engage in business and make a profit.' Yet you do not know what your life will be like tomorrow. You are just a vapor that appears for a little while and then vanishes away. Instead, you ought to say, 'If the Lord wills, we shall live and also do this or that'" (*New American Standard Bible*, James 4:13-15).

BRANDING

With the marketplace drowning in sameness, a powerful brand--built not on a degree or on a university diploma but on a value proposition statement--has become a competitive necessity. Or stated differently, the bottom line for everyone comes down to a choice: "to be distinct or extinct." [Ferrazzi, p. 226]

If branding is so important, how does one brand them self? What does a personal branding message look like? How is a brand statement used? Let me try and answer these and other related questions by setting forth the following points:

1. The Owner of Your Brand
   You cannot expect someone else to define who you are. You cannot depend upon someone else to influence other people's personal and professional expectations of who you are. You cannot expect your parents to define you. Your career is yours and yours alone to manage.

2. The Characteristics of Your Brand

   Now that <u>you</u> have chosen to be the owner of your brand, what should your brand look like? That is, what are the characteristics of your brand?

   o The construction of your brand starts with your passions. What are you passionate about? Are you passionate about innovation? Are you passionate about transformation? Are you passionate about collaboration? Make that a part of your brand.

   o The construction of your brand continues with skills and/or character qualities that are demanded by the marketplace. If the marketplace is demanding creativity, make that a part of your brand. If the marketplace is demanding servant leadership, make that a part of your brand. If the marketplace is demanding integrity, make that a part of your plan.

   o Finally, the construction of your brand must make you appear to be multi-faceted. Your brand should not make a single claim. You need to have a brand that makes two or three claims (think of an explorer or an Oklahoma sooner).

3. The Qualities of Your Brand

   Now that you have identified the characteristics of your brand, what are the qualities of your brand? The best brands, like the most intriguing people, have three qualities.

   o First, a brand should be unique. It should have a distinct message. You want to be the brown egg in a carton of white eggs!

   o Second, to become a great brand, your brand must be seen as being relentlessly focused on delivering value. In fact, your brand should always be stated in terms of what you will do for others!

   o Third, you are to be an ambassador. We read in the New Testament: "Therefore, we are ambassadors for Christ, God making his appeal through us. We implore you on behalf of Christ, be reconciled to God" (*New American Standard Bible*, 2 Corinthians 5:20).

4. The Packaging of Your Brand
   Your brand statement must be relevant. It must resonate with future employers. And it must be real.

5. The Authentication of Your Brand
   To authenticate your brand statement, you need to identify five-to-seven success stories that support your brand statement. These success stories should in crafted in terms of how you increased revenues, decreased expenses, increased efficiencies, and/or diminished risks (using dollars and percentages).

Objections--"I don't have enough experience to build a brand! I am not sure what I want to do when I graduate! My only job has been flipping burgers at Mickey D's!" This is the point! You need to start building your brand now. You need to determine your passions. You need to learn what the market wants. You need to assess what you are good at..... And the good news is that you have four years to do so. Don't waste your four years in college.

CONNECTING

Now that you have defined who you are, determined what makes you unique, and packaged that into a brand statement--that is, you have characterized yourself--it is time to connect with others. It is time to network! To better enable you to connect with others, let me address five questions about networking.

1. What is connecting?
   It is the process of sharing your knowledge and resources, time and energy, friends and associates, and empathy and compassion in a continual effort to provide value to others, while coincidentally increasing the value of your network. [Ferrazzi, p. 8]

2. Why should one connect?

   o One should connect, first, because you can't get there alone.

- o Second, networks are like muscles--the more you work them, the stronger they become. [Ferrazzi, p. 19] Too often, we get caught up in focusing solely on the work that will get us through the day. We are too busy! The idea isn't to find us another environment tomorrow--be it a new job or a new career--but to be constantly creating the community that enables us to find a new job (or a new career), no matter what may occur.
- o Third, we are to place the interests of others in front of ourselves. When the disciples asked Jesus--"Teacher, which is the greatest commandment in the Law?"--Jesus did not hesitate. He replied: "Love the Lord your God with all your heart and with all your soul and with all your mind. This is the first and greatest commandment. And the second is like it: Love your neighbor as yourself" (*New American Standard Bible*, Matthew 22:36-39). We can go through life focused on ourselves. We can go through life expecting others to serve us. We can go through life never connecting. And if we do--it will be a very miserable and unfulfilling life. That is because there always is greater joy in placing the interests of others in front of ourselves.

3. What does one share when networking?
Tim Sanders nails this answer in his wonderful book, *Love is the Killer App*. We are to share our:

- o knowledge,
- o network, and
- o compassion. [Sanders, p. 13]

4. Who do you network with?
Everyone! You include every member of your fraternity/sorority, fellow employees, high school friends you stay in contact with, teachers and professors, pastors and counselors, and even parents of your close friends. Adding individuals to your network works best when it's done with the under-lying philosophy that every person is potentially relevant to you and your network.

Objections -- "Are you serious, I don't have time to network! I don't have any knowledge that is worth sharing with others? I don't know influential people that I can connect with others! I have no interest in sharing my compassion with someone who is struggling! I am a college student!" And the answer to all of these objections is--you are wrong! You have four years to acquire knowledge that can be shared with others. You have four years to build and nurture a network that will make finding a job easier. You have four years to learn how to be compassionate. Failing to invest in building a network while you are in college will make finding a job in your chosen career daunting.

MARKETING

Now that you have branded yourself and have built a network--it is time to market yourself.

1. What are some marketing suggestions?

   o First, develop a thirty-second speech (the infamous elevator speech) that explains your brand.
   o Second, incorporate the text of this thirty-second speech into your résumé, your LinkedIn profile, and your bio (if you create one).
   o Third, dedicate the top-half of the first page of your résumé to your brand statement and some of the killer success stories that authenticate your brand statement.
   o Finally, create a blog site (or even better, a web site) that serves as a marketing tool to clearly articulate your brand.

2. What are some of the traps to avoid when marketing your brand?

   o Avoid the trap of falling asleep at the wheel. When it comes to marketing your brand, you have to be on your game—twenty-four hours a day, seven days a week 365 days a year!

- o Be careful how you dress when you go to the mall. You may never know who in your network you might meet there!
- o Be careful what you post on your Facebook account. Someone might stumble across some rather embarrassing or compromising pictures. You want to appear to be intelligent and mature. You do not want to be seen as a partier.
- o Be careful what you choose to use as your voice mail greeting. Potential employers do not need to hear--"Hey man, this is Alex. I can't come to the phone right now because I am wasted. I will get back with you when I wake up."

3. How often do you market to your network?
Continually. Don't go dark on your network. The number one objective in marketing your network is to remember a simple rule: "Above all, never, ever disappear." [Ferrazzi, p. 94]

4. How often do you update your résumé?
Update your résumé (and bio) on a regular basis. Every time you take on a new job, project, or responsibility--update your résumé. Every time you earn a degree, an award, or a certificate--update your résumé. One of the most important reasons for doing this, is because it provides you with a barometer of how your brand building is progressing.

Objection--"Hey, I am at college to have fun!" While it is hard to build a successful brand image, it is virtually impossible to do so if you choose to try and market a brand image of immaturity, drinking, and debauchery. I am not saying that you can't have fun at college. What I am trying to encourage you to consider is that everything you do in college will either help or hurt your future search for a job.

CONCLUSION

In conclusion, I want to encourage you to invest in your future during your college years. Begin now building your brand and your value proposition for future employers. Begin now building your network, which is your gift to others. Begin now marketing your brand that proclaims to all what you can do for others. It is a journey that will prove to be both enlightening and enjoyable.

APPENDIX #5

THE TEN COMMANDMENTS OF SPEAKING

What are the basic elements one has to master to be an effective public speaker? What does one need to focus on to improve their speaking skills? How does one effectively broadcast their brand? The following quick primer is the result of much study, instruction, and practice. I have cast them in terms of commandments. These ten commandments of public speaking should make it more understandable, relevant, and actionable.

o #1 – Thou shalt know thy audience.
   Thom Singer writes in *The ABC's of Speaking* (a must-have for your library): "Before you accept an offer to speak, ask about the makeup of the audience. Age, gender, occupations, backgrounds, job titles, purpose of the group, and their expectations are part of the information you need to prepare. While many people who speak infrequently have a standard speech that they give, you must be sure that you customize your remarks to the demographics and needs of the individual audience. The more you understand about whom will be hearing you speak, the better you can tailor your presentation to create a connection with the group. Think about those who will sit in

the uncomfortable chairs and make them the priority." [Singer, *The ABC's of* Speaking, 77]

o   #2 – Thou shalt know thy purpose.
In his best-selling book, *7 Habits of Highly Effective People,* Stephen Covey tells us to "begin with the end in mind." [Covey, *7 Habits of Highly Effective People*, p. 99] Too many people take on a speaking assignment with no specific purpose in mind. Others jump in and try to wing it. Before you speak, take a few moments (at least!) and focus on the purpose of your speech. Singer writes: "Are you there to educate? To inform? To entertain? To tell a story? To motivate? To influence or encourage those listening? To deliver good or bad news? Is your presentation designed as a call to action for others? What is your personal motivation for being the person speaking?..... Know why you are there and be intentional in everything you do with regards to your presentation." [Singer, pp. 37-38]

o   #3 – Thou shalt know that language matters.
In his best-selling book, *Axiom: Powerful Leadership Proverbs*, Bill Hybels writes: "Leaders rise and fall by the language they use. Sometimes whole visions live or die on the basis of the words the leader chooses for articulating that vision. When you put the right words to a vision or a principle, it becomes axiomatic. It begins to live! It becomes memorable and powerful.....The very best leaders I know wrestle with words until they are able to communicate their big ideas in a way that captures the imagination, catalyzes action, and lifts spirits. They coin creeds and fashion slogans and creates rallying cries, all because they understand that language matters." [Hybels, *Axiom: Powerful Leadership* Proverbs, p. 17] For example, when Willow Creek was setting forth a strategic vision for members of the church, one of their key values was compassion. Instead of saying they were going to be compassionate (big yawn), they said they were going to "unleash unprecedented amounts of compassion into our broken world." [Hybels, p. 19] Which do you think is more effective?

o   #4 – Thou shalt not be monotone.

The only thing worse than listening to a boring speaker, is to listen to a monotone speaker. Speaking to an audience in a monotone voice is the quickest way to ensure that the audience tunes you out. Your content may even be outstanding but outstanding content delivered in a flat, monotone voice ensures that you will be an ineffective speaker. Your speech should include voice inflection (soft segments as well as louder segments), enthusiasm, energy, a change in pacing (faster and slower segments), and clear enunciation (be willing to even emphasize individual syllables).

o   #5 – Thou shalt avoid all verbal tics.

Thom Singer writes: "Many who are nervous or inexperienced about speaking in front of an audience are scared of pauses, and they fill in the gaps with filler words--ummm, ahhh, you know, etc. They often do not know they are doing it, and have no idea how the continuous use of such 'verbal tics' can cause the audience to lose track of their message." [Singer, p. 78] There are several ways to know if you are making this type of mistake. First, you can have a friend grade you as you speak. Second, you can record your speech. Or third, you can video tape your speech. If you determine that your speech is full of verbal tics, practice reducing those verbal tics in your everyday speech. You may be surprised how this will aid your public speaking proficiency. And remember--do not be scared of a pause in your speech, even if you are searching for a word. Pauses are much shorter than they seem and can even be used for emphasis.

o   #6 – Thou shalt not have thy feet in concrete.

Do not forget to walk around while you are speaking. Nobody wants to watch a statue speak. Use as much space as you can. Get out from behind the podium. Walk into the crowd. Look into the eyes of the audience. Use movement to your advantage.

o   #7 – Thou shalt not flail like a duck.

Thom Singer writes: "Specific and well-planned movements will express a powerful thought and help you make a lasting connection with the audience. However, stiff and awkward gestures distract from your expertise and make you appear like a novice, nervous, and uncomfortable." [Singer, p. 30] Gestures can be one of the most powerful tools in your speaking arsenal. They can be used to draw attention to an important point. They can be used to emphasize an important fact. They can be used to visualize an important point. Just remember they can also detract from your presentation. Use them judiciously and wisely.

o   #8 – Thou shalt use stories in your presentations.
The greatest teacher of all time, Jesus Christ, largely taught in parables. Why? People easily remember stories. Embrace story-telling in your presentations. Whenever possible, frame your presentation with a single story. Whenever possible, illustrate key points with stories. Whenever possible, use stories in your introduction and conclusion. This takes work but it will make your presentation more effective and memorable. One other side note--include humor and wit in your stories. The audience is not expecting you to be a stand-up comedian (and you should avoid trying to become one). Learn the difference between telling jokes and adding observational humor to your stories and presentations.

o   #9 – Thou shalt memorize (a part of) your speech.
There is nothing worse than sitting in an audience listening to a speaker read their speech. Why don't they just pass it out! Being a visual learner, I would prefer that! I am not suggesting that you memorize your whole speech. I am suggesting that you memorize your opening, your key stories, and your closing. This enables you to start strong, drive home your key points, and finish with a bang. If you want to be an effective speaker, adherence to just this commandment will enable you to impact your audience. It allows you to give them several memorable moments.

o   #10 – Thou shalt be personal.
Thom Singer writes: "Show your audience your personal side, even in a business presentation. Expose pieces of your personal life and

your past mistakes and vulnerabilities, as this will make you easier for the average person to relate to you as a human being." [Singer, p. 55] Speakers too often think that they have to appear as an authoritative expert. They think that being personal diminishes their effectiveness as a speaker. Nothing could be further from the truth. Authenticity is what makes an audience connect to a speaker.

There you go! This is not an exhaustive list of items one needs to become an effective speaker. It is merely a starting point. Just know that if one masters these ten commandments, one will greatly elevate one's speaking prowess and will be a long way down the road to speaking expertise.

WORKS CITED

Sal Bommarito, *22 of the Best Dos Equis "The Most Interesting Man in the World Quotes*. Policymic, July, 2012.
http://www.policymic.com/articles/9659/22-of-the-best-dos-equis-the-most-interesting-man-in-the-world-quotes-video

Scott Brinker, *Five New Skills for the Future of Marketing*. Chief Marketing Technologist, February 23, 2009.
http://www.chiefmartec.com/2009/02/5-new-skills-for-the-future-of-marketing.html

Stephen Covey, *7 Habits of Highly Effective People*. Simon & Schuster, New York, 2004. Print.

James Marshall Crotty, *60% of College Grads Can't Find Work in Their Field. Is a Management Degree the Answer?* Forbes.com, March 1, 2012.
http://www.forbes.com/sites/jamesmarshallcrotty/2012/03/01/most-college-grads-cant-find-work-in-their-field-is-a-management-degree-the-answer/

Bonnie Dangel, *Resume Renovation*.
http://bondanservices.com

Keith Ferrazzi, *Never Eat Alone: And Other Secrets to Success, One Relationship At a Time*. Currency-Doubleday, New York, 2005. Print.

Wayne D. Ford, Ph.D, *The Accelerated Job Search*. The Management Advantage, Inc., Walnut Creek, 1999. Print.

Huffington Post, *Résumé Design Eye Tracking Study*. Huffingtonpost.com, May 9, 2012.
http://www.huffingtonpost.com/2012/05/09/résumé-design-eye-tracking-study-6-seconds_n_1503037.html).

Bill Hybels, Axiom: Powerful Leadership Proverbs. Zondervan, Grand Rapids, 2008. Print.

Oklahoma Historical Society, *Oklahoma Historical Society's Encyclopedia of Oklahoma History & Culture: Land Run of 1889*. http://digital.library.okstate.edu/encyclopedia/entries/L/LA014.html

Tom Peters, *Circle of Innovation: You Can't Shrink Your Way to Greatness*. Vintage Books, New York, 1999. Print.

Resume Doctor, *Top Questions Asked at Job Interviews*. ResumeDoctor.com. http://www.resumedoctor.com/resourcecenter.htm#interviewsurvey

Tim Sanders, *Love is the Killer App: How Win Business and Influence Friends*. Three River Press, New York, 2002. Print.

Tim Sinclair, *Branded: Sharing Jesus with a Consumer Culture*. Kregel Publications, Grand Rapids, 2011. Print.

Thom Singer, *The ABC's of Speaking*. New Year Publishing, Danville, 2010. Print.

Roman Turski, *The Evaders: Secrets and Spies: Behind-the-Scenes Stories of World War II*. Readers Digest Association, Pleasantville, 1964. Print.

www.ingramcontent.com/pod-product-compliance
Lightning Source LLC
Chambersburg PA
CBHW030807180526
45163CB00003B/1172